Citizens DisUnited:

Passive Investors, Drone CEOs, and the Corporate Capture of the American Dream

Bob Monks

Citizens DisUnited:

Passive Investors, Drone CEOs, and the Corporate Capture of the American Dream

Robert A.G. Monks

Miniver Press

To Melinda

Contents

Introduction

When the freedom they wished for most was freedom from responsibility, then Athens ceased to be free and was never free again.

— Edith Hamilton

This book is a warning, a plea for involvement, and a call to arms.

Democratic capitalism—the source of America's vast wealth, the foundation of our entire economic system—is threatened as never before in my eighty years, not from without but from within. Shareholders today no longer own, except in the narrowest legal sense, the corporations they have invested in. Emboldened by the Supreme Court and enabled by a compliant Congress and compromised regulators, America's CEOs have staged a corporate coup d'état. They, not the titular owners of the businesses, decide where and how company resources will be deployed, what laws will be evaded in the pursuit of short-term gain, what offshore havens profits will be stashed in to avoid taxation, and critically, how lavishly the CEOs themselves will be compensated.

A decade ago, at an annual meeting of the ExxonMobil Corporation, I addressed then-CEO and board chairman Lee Raymond as "Emperor." He had, after all, all the trappings of an absolute ruler, including the ability to utterly control the proceedings at this supposedly "democratic" interface between ExxonMobil and its shareholders. Back then, I thought of Raymond as something of an outlier among chief executives. Today, his type is commonplace. Far too much of American business is being run for the personal enrichment and glorification of its manager-kings.

1

This book will show how and why that is so. It will also unveil, for the first time, a new study showing that corporations "un-owned" by their shareholders—what I term corporate "drones"—are far worse corporate citizens *and* have significantly lower average shareholder returns than firms in which owners still exercise authority over management. Manager-kings, it turns out, are bad both for society and for business itself.

Seven decades ago, Adolph A. Berle warned that granting managers free rein posed the "danger of a corporate oligarchy coupled with the probability of an era of corporate plundering."[1] Both fears have been fulfilled in our own time, but this takeover hasn't happened in a vacuum. Passive index funds, algorithm trading, the incessant churn of financial markets around the world have all served to weaken the bonds of ownership and divorce shareholders from any compelling sense of responsibility for the corporations in which they have invested.

That must change if the plundering is to stop. It must change if America is again to be seen as a trustworthy place to do business. (That the United States ranked 19th among global countries on Transparency International's 2012 Corruption Perceptions Index should be a source of national shame) [2]. But this change can be led only by the Great and Good of Investing—the leading foundations and university endowments, the vast public employee pension funds, the colossal index funds that hold an ever-increasing share of the national wealth. Again, in this book I will show why that is so, and I will propose several ways in which the trustees of these foundations and funds can begin to reassert ownership and fulfill responsibilities too long neglected. In investing as in government, the price of freedom is eternal vigilance.

Though I have tried hard to leave myself out of the account to follow, this is also a highly personal tale—the summing up of a lifetime's journey.

The cultural anthropology of the Boston Brahmin into which I was born eight decades ago included primogeniture (males only), Harvard, charitable commitments, and wealth, in Boston amounts.

One's place in this universe was determined by birth, not through merit. But make no mistake, one was entitled! It took many years to understand that my innate discomfort was based on the conviction that there is something wrong with such privilege without engagement, something wrong with ownership without responsibility.

While in college I felt the need to earn my way out of the Brahmin mold, and so each summer I headed west to work on heavy construction—pipeline jobs that paid enough to cover my own tuition. I seem to have intuited Malcolm Gladwell's rule about success, that it requires 10,000 hours of application to any learning activity, even the most primitive. In my case, the application came on the Charles River, where I devoted four hours a day over four years to pulling an oar through the water as hard and as long as possible. [3]

This simple discipline gave me a strong sense of worth. That plus earning my own keep also gave me the confidence to ask Milly to marry me. She said yes, and we took care of the formalities two weeks after graduation. Thus, according to the value system of my little world, I had achieved in full measure what was expected of me. But I also felt I had earned the right to question that which made no sense. All in all, I was restless.

During my years of preparation, the local wasp-o-cracy treated me very well, among other respects, in being a partner (maybe the youngest ever) in a respected law firm and, later, chairman of one of the most prestigious local banks, Ralph Lowell's bank, at a time when Lowells and Cabots still counted greatly in Boston. And yet, I had a gnawing discomfort. Maybe it was being consigned to status without reference to my merits. Just as likely, my unease arose from being part of an established class confident of its integrity and certain that society was being run for its unique benefit.

Having rejected the inheritance of medicine (both grandfathers) and the church (my father) and having arrived near enough the top as lawyer, banker, businessman, public servant—and having failed as a candidate for public office (the U.S. Senate, from Maine)—I abandoned conventional career paths and forged from my interests, capabilities, and instincts a challenging and fulfilling life.

3

For more than thirty years my thoughts and energies have been devoted to the global effort of harmonizing the energy, creativity, and wealth-generating capability of a greed-based corporate system with the needs and interests of society. I've worked inside government: on deregulation for the first President Bush; in the Labor Department, developing the rules of shareholder activism for employee benefit plans; as one of the founding trustees of what is now the largest institutional investor in the United States, the Thrift Investment Board for federal employees; and as a founding director of the federally owned United States Synthetic Fuels Corporation.

As a businessman, in addition to my Boston banking career, I've been CEO of a coal and oil firm as well as the founder of four companies in the corporate governance field, most notably Institutional Shareholder Services (ISS), the nation's leading proxy advisory firm. I've served as a director, among others, of Westmoreland Coal Company, Penn Virginia Company, Esterline Corporation, Boston Safe Deposit & Trust Company, Codex Corporation (merged into what was then Motorola Corporation), Mitsubishi Corporation-US, Hermes Focus Asset Management Company (as Vice Chairman), Banque Bruxelles Lambert, and Tyco—until I was asked to leave the board for, in essence, seeking to hold management accountable for its actions.

I have testified before congressional committees on many occasions and before state legislative committees widely. I've also published a dozen books, including most recently *Corpocracy*, and maintain an extensive website with appendices of my writings over the last thirty years at www.ragm.com.

As the old fellow in East Machias used to say, "What you see depends on where you sit." As the above suggests, I have sat many different places and thus have had a vast range of perspective, all of which compels every effort to preserve the integrity of the corporate system and the wealth-creating properties of the "equity culture," both of which are desperately at risk.

The increasing dominion of corporate values over those of flesh-and-blood human beings has become pervasive. Whether it is a bitterly won battle to achieve universal health care at the cost of locking in private sector profits, or the unlimited and undisclosed disbursement of corporate funds throughout the electoral, legislative, regulatory, and judicial elements of our "free society," the evidence of corporate hegemony is universal and undeniable. Nor is it possible to ignore the reality that the traditional restraints on corporate power have proven largely fictitious and ultimately unavailing.

Where are the owners, and in particular the leaders among them? Shirking obvious duty is harmful in its own right, but refusing to act because doing so would be distracting or otherwise inconvenient is doubly injurious. Not only does it deprive ownership of needed participants; an unwillingness to act also dilutes the legitimacy of any effort by other owners to require accountability.

This book, finally, is by way of a plea—atonement for my own shame—that those fortunate and able enough to prosper in our society stop taking the "commons" for granted, and begin committing their time, values, and integrity, to the functioning of companies of which they are owners. We need the involvement of those considered as leaders. More to the point, we must have their effective participation if we are to avoid descent into a permanent corporatist state—and we are today at the very edge of that abyss.

****

1.
Capture!

America's corporations today enjoy an absolute reign. They and they alone have the power to control the rules under which they function. They have the first say on the allocation of public resources, and they have exempted themselves from nearly all financial obligations to the nation and its people. This is not a prediction of what's to come. This is the present state of affairs, the America we live in right now.

Corporations are complex mechanisms made up of shareholders, employees, goods and services, even customers. Structurally, management is only a small part of the whole, but it is here — in the top rank of management — that this coup d'état has been staged. The most powerful CEOs have effectively seized authority over a vast range of America's corporate resources, and through those resources over the nation itself, without assuming any of the responsibilities of dominion.

The case will be made in full in the chapters that follow. Below, an introduction to the principal ways in which corporate power has captured America.

  • *The financial power of American corporations now controls every stage of politics — executive, legislative, and judicial.*

In its January 2010 decision in the *Citizens United* case, the Supreme Court not only affirmed the "personhood" of corporations; it also effectively removed all legal restraints on the extent of corporate financial involvement in politics, a grotesque decision that can have only one effect: maximizing corporate — *not national* — value.

Having been granted extraordinary power to direct unlimited corporate funds to political objectives entirely in their own self-interest, and an extraordinarily efficient vehicle for doing so in the newly created Super PACs, business has been understandably quick to the starting line. Total outside spending—that is, spending not overtly on behalf of a particular candidate—on the 2008 presidential election ran to $286 million. Outside spending on the 2012 election topped that figure by early September on its way to a final tally of $1.176 billion, a four-fold growth in only four years. [4]

And this, it must be pointed out, is only the money required to have some sort of ID tag eventually attached to it. Super PACs get to hide their donors until the election is over and the damage done. Then they have to fess up. But, 501(c)(6) trade associations and 501(c)(4) "social welfare organizations" (which, despite their tag, are allowed by the IRS to devote a substantial portion of their activities to "influencing legislation by propaganda or otherwise"), operate under no such minimal obligations. These groups need *never* provide a breakdown of their donors, and here the money flow is of tsunami proportions.

In 2010, 501(c)(6)s and (4)s together are estimated to have outspent Super PACs by greater than 2 to 1. The U.S. Chamber of Commerce alone accounted for nearly 25 percent of total trade association and social welfare organization spending in 2010, nearly all of it from corporations able to cloak their individual identities.[5] And "cloak" here is the key word, despite the majority's insistence in *Citizens United* that the decision was all about transparency.

Between 1990 and 2006, the percentage of outside spending with no identifiable donors rarely topped 10 percent. In 2008, phantom donors reached 25 percent; in 2010, they topped 40 percent. The Center for Responsive Politics has yet to estimate the figure for 2012, but this is not likely to be a downward trend. We could be facing permanent election cycles in which 50 percent or more of all outside funding comes from unidentified sources, a condition fundamentally at odds with the most basic principles not just of transparency but of democratic rule itself.[6]

What's true of presidential politics is equally applicable at the congressional level. Between 2000 and 2012, total spending on all House races nearly doubled to $1.1 billion. Meanwhile, total spending on Senate races climbed from $410 million in 2008 to $700 million four years later, and none of the largest contributions was disinterested money.

In 2010, the campaign committee of then-House Minority Leader John Boehner raised $9.8 million, in large part because Boehner was almost certain to become House Speaker the following January. His three biggest donors that year were a who's who of supplicants for regulatory relief and favorable legislative treatment: AT&T; Massey Energy, Ohio-based and the nation's largest privately owned coal company; and First Energy, also Ohio-based and then under order to pay $1.5 billion to settle a lawsuit brought by EPA alleging the company had failed to install pollution control equipment in its upgraded coal-fired plants. Two years later, now House Speaker and standing for reelection virtually uncontested, Boehner more than doubled his 2010 take, raising nearly $22 million. His top three donors again included AT&T, Massey Energy, and First Energy. Among other top ten contributors: Paulson & Co., once the world's largest hedge fund but now with its assets cut nearly in half, and American Electric Power, 60 percent coal-dependent and fighting an effort by the Ohio utilities commission to "accelerate the move to full competition."[7]

At the state level, the raw power of money to influence legislation is even greater. The grandly named American Legislative Exchange Council in theory brings state legislatures and corporate interests together on an equal footing to discuss topics of mutual interest. In practice, legislators pay $50 a year to belong to the Council, while corporate membership can run $25,000 annually, plus additional expenditures if a corporate representative wants to buy a seat on one of ALEC's task forces—and who wouldn't, since that's where "model legislation" is most likely to get written, bills that will then be carried back to states and thrown into the hopper for a vote. For the three years ending in 2011, ALEC's corporate component paid $21.6 million in dues, while its state legislator component ponied up about $250,000— a ratio roughly of 86 to 1—, and all that needs to be said about the balance of power and flow of interests within the organization.[8]

9

Political power, political influence, political direction—they are all for sale in America today, on the block for the highest bidder but at an auction only a few Americans can afford to attend. In 2012, the top 100 donors contributed 57 percent of the $834 million raised by Super PACs of all ideological stripes—$474 million in all, almost 60 percent of that to conservative causes. True, Republicans did not triumph in 2012, at least at the national level, but politicians of all persuasions are drawn to money as deer are drawn to salt licks, and the more the richest Americans are allowed to give, the greater will be their influence over both parties and the national political life generally.[9]

In this context, the defense of *Citizens United* offered by Justice Samuel Alito at a November 2012 meeting of the archconservative Federalist Society borders on the clinically obtuse or borderline deranged. "The question is whether speech that goes to the very heart of government should be limited to certain preferred corporations—namely, media corporations," Alito said. "Surely the idea that the First Amendment protects only certain privileged voices should be disturbing to anybody who believes in free speech." Is the arch battle of American politics really over whether, say, News Corp.'s Rupert Murdoch or Exxon's Rex Tillerson gets the better podium?[10]

Here is the political world the Supreme Court (or a 5-4 majority thereof) has bequeathed unto us. By granting corporations a political voice, by failing to restrain the resources to amplify and enshrine its reach, and by simply shutting individuals of anything less than stupendous wealth out of the equation, the Court has effectively created a virtuous circle, but only for those inside it.

- *Capture has been further implemented through the extensive lobbying power of corporations.*

Money in and of itself buys nothing. Something has to be for sale and the two entities, buyer and seller, need a means of coming together in mutual interest—i.e., the lobbying industry.

Abraham Lincoln's mostly forgotten warning about "corporations . . . enthroned" and Dwight Eisenhower's famous caution about the "unwarranted influence by the military-industrial complex" have both been fully realized in our own time. Reported lobbying expenditures have risen annually, to $3.5 billion in 2010. Half of the senators and 42 percent of House members who left Congress between 1998 and 2004 became lobbyists, as did 310 former appointees of George W. Bush, and 283 of Bill Clinton.[11]

Money buys voices, ears, face time, and sit-downs, but it also buys silence, in multiple ways. Witness health care: So thoroughly has the insurance industry captured Congress that neither the Obama administration nor its legislative supporters could even seriously mention a system of "single payer" insurance, much less bring it to the House or Senate floor for a vote. Meanwhile, business lobbyists were quietly assuring that whatever program of "universal coverage" did emerge would lock in the interests of the insurance and the pharmaceutical industries. (Indeed, only a regulatory filing error laid bare the fact that Aetna Insurance had donated $4 million to the U.S. Chamber of Commerce in 2011, gigantically in excess of the $100,000 in Chamber dues it reported in 2010.)[12]

History has yet to sort out whether the second Iraq War served any national objectives beyond military and industrial ones, but the suspicion that oil interests played a critical role in the rush to battle is enhanced by former Vice President Dick Cheney's continuing refusal, more than a decade later, to reveal the names of the participants in his energy transition committee.[13] Simultaneously, the inability to force public disclosure of those participants offers a window into how thoroughly the energy industry controls its own agenda, destiny, and information flow. Not only has the industry succeeded in achieving and maintaining special regulatory and tax treatment; in multiple other ways, it functions as an independent state.

One more sign of the ascendancy of influence peddling: the casualness with which so much of it goes on these days. The Romney campaign on Wednesday evening of the 2012 Republican National Convention hosted its major donors—those who had given or raised $1 million or more —aboard the *Cracker Bay*, a 150-foot yacht owned by Florida developer Gary Morse. And as if to prove that in today's America money talks but doesn't have to listen, the *Cracker Bay* was flying not the stars and stripes of America, but the merchant flag of the

Cayman Islands.

Shameless? Perhaps not entirely. ABC News, which caught wind of the event even though it appeared on no official schedule, reported that most attendees covered their name tags as they exited the yacht. But the scene calls to mind not so much embarrassment as the way Mafia dons used to cover their faces with fedoras as they walked out of war councils.[14]

- *As much as corporations have captured America,
CEOs have captured the power and riches of American
corporations.*

The nexus of influence and cash is nothing new in American politics or in political life generally, nor is it now or has ever been ideology-centric. Robber barons papered both houses of Congress and both sides of their aisles with money at the close of the 19th century. At the height of his power, J.P. Morgan functioned for all practical purposes as America's central bank, the court of last resort in times of crisis, with all the leverage such a position entailed. As the embodiment of American wealth, corporations are at one level simply treading long-established ground. What's new is where this nexus of influence and cash is now situated within corporations: CEOs, the people presumably paid by the real owners to run them, although the most compelling evidence available — money — would suggest otherwise.

Total U.S. CEO compensation has grown more than seven-fold since 1978, far in excess of stock market growth over the same period. [15] Why? No metric justifies such a raid on the corporate treasury and shareholder equity. There's absolutely no evidence that such a soaring pay curve is based on economic value added. Indeed, the only possible explanation for such spectacular growth is the simplest one available: CEOs control the levers of power within almost all major American corporations and, as such, can pay themselves essentially whatever they damn well please.

Part of this CEO self-largess results from the artful manipulation and exploitation of the U.S. tax code, but the larger part by far can be found in the performance contracts that CEOs, unfettered by dissenting voices within the boardroom, effectively write for themselves. On the surface, these contracts are geared to performance, and thus should represent a win-win for management and investors. In practice, the performance is so "un-indexed" against meaningful benchmarks and measured across so short a term that only one winner is sure to emerge: management.

Harvard Business School professor Mihir Desai took up this subject in an interview with the *Harvard Business Review*:

"High quality managers and investors should be richly rewarded. My problem is not with the *level* of compensation, it's with the *form*. Contracts that don't measure performance relative to appropriate benchmarks or that claim to disentangle luck from skill over short horizons can do more harm than good . . . . The remarkable wealth obtainable simply by influencing short-run outcomes distorts people into decisions that are not in the interest of the long-run shareholder."

Elsewhere in the interview, Desai says that "the twin crises of modern American capitalism—rising income inequality and repeated governance crises (including the financial crisis)—can be traced in part to the proliferation of these very high-powered incentive contracts for managers and institutional investors."[16]

He's right, of course, but Desai fails to mention the larger crisis of modern American capitalism inherent in the situation he described, that it is increasingly a one-way street meant to serve the appetites of CEOs with little or no regard for the nominal "owners" of the corporations or the larger needs of society.

• *Having captured corporate power, CEOs are systematically externalizing corporate liabilities.*

During the same period that CEOs were doubling their own compensation, the "best" CEOs of the "best" companies abrogated the century-old commitment by employers to provide pensions to their workers. IBM was the corporate leader in abolishing a "real" pension system for its employees. The 2006 elimination of ongoing defined benefit plans at Big Blue was touted as saving the company as much as $3 billion while providing it with a more predictable cost structure, but the key message went unspoken: The risk of retirement now resided with the individual, not the company—first at IBM, and then broadly across the corporate landscape. Meanwhile, the principal beneficiaries of the one-time boost to the bottom line brought about by these epic transferences were—no surprise—the CEOs who instigated them.[17]

Tobacco companies have long externalized the known health costs of their products, both to the consumers and to society at large in those cases where tobacco users cannot pay for their own health care costs. More recently, energy companies have externalized the costs of environmental degradation by effectively pre-building fines and other penalties into their pricing structures. And, of course, there's the Holy Grail of externalization: Too Big to Fail, an appalling concept that rewards morbid corporate obesity by shifting all the risks of mismanagement, no matter how gross, to taxpayers, while failing to hold the executives responsible for that mismanagement to even the least standards of competent stewardship.

This is the essence of "capture"—CEOs are enriched, while all other corporate constituencies, including government, are left with liabilities. A relatively few autocrats have seized control of the policies and wealth of the United States.

- *Capture has placed the most powerful CEOs above the reach of the law and beyond its effective enforcement.*

Extensive evidence of Wall Street's critical involvement in the 2007-08 financial crisis notwithstanding, one could count almost on a single hand the number of senior Wall Street executives removed for cause at surviving firms. What's more, pay levels have been rigorously maintained even when, as noted earlier, TARP payments had to be refinanced in order to remove any possible restrictions.

While several financial firms have paid civil penalties for their abuses, the amounts involved bear little relation to the malfeasance. U.S. District Judge Jed S. Rakoff recently—and rightly—rejected the $285 million settlement agreed to between Citigroup Inc. and the

Securities and Exchange Commission as "neither fair, nor reasonable, nor adequate, nor in the public interest."[18]

Worse, such fines as have been imposed on the financial industry are basically being paid by the government itself. At the same time that various regulatory agencies boast of record-setting penalties assessed against banks, the Federal Reserve pays banks interest on money that is not being lent, resulting in an "interest margin" in excess of $12 billion realized by U.S. banks since the start of the decade—more than ample funding for any penalties suffered.[19]

> • *Capture has been further perpetuated through the removal of property "off shore," where it is neither regulated nor taxed.*

The social contract between Americans and their corporations was supposed to go as follows: In exchange for limited liability and other privileges, corporations were to be held to a set of obligations that legitimatized the powers they were given. But modern corporations have assumed the right to relocate to different jurisdictions, almost at will, irrespective of where they really do business, and thus avoid the constraints of those obligations.

Not surprisingly, the biggest winners within these new, stateless, pick-your-own-address corporations have been CEOs, who by and large decide where the firm's hat will officially be hung and where its profits will be parked. A new report from the Institute for Policy Studies matched corporate taxes paid with the 100 highest-compensated American executives. Of those CEOs, 26 received more in total annual compensation in 2011 than their companies paid in total corporate taxes. Collectively, these 26 companies have 537 subsidiaries in tax havens such as the Cayman Islands, Bermuda, and Gibraltar—an average of 20-plus subsidiaries per firm. The subsidiaries, in turn, allow the corporations to assign profits to minimal tax jurisdictions while claiming losses from U.S. operations. And, of course, all this is perfectly legal under a U.S. tax code that has been largely crafted by industry lobbyists.[20]

As Nicholas Shaxson writes of modern corporations in *Treasure*

Islands, "The privileges have been preserved and enhanced, but the obligations have withered." Meanwhile, the U.S. Treasury is estimated to be losing $100 billion annually from offshore tax abuses.[21]

- *Capture extends to the regulatory agencies as well.*

In early 2010, Alabama Rep. Spencer Bachus, the incoming chairman of the House Financial Services Committee, caused a stir when he told an interviewer: "In Washington, the view is that the banks are to be regulated, and my view is that Washington and the regulators are there to serve the banks."[22] A little over two years later, the public barely blinked when a majority of the Securities and Exchange Commission's five members yielded to pressure from the money-market mutual funds industry and blocked a reform measure that might have forestalled a taxpayer bailout like the one that saved the industry during the 2008 financial crisis—a bailout, by the way, that had taxpayers on the hook for $3 trillion, four times the size of the much more celebrated TARP rescue operation.[23]

More than forty years ago, University of Chicago economist and later Nobel laureate George Stigler, warned of what he called "regulatory capture"—a condition in which industries wind up imprisoning the agencies that are supposed to regulate them. Such capture has been fully achieved in our own time, and nowhere more so than in the financial industry. Indeed, the finance sector has effectively captured the capture.[24]

The leading finance sector firms and CEOs—and their hired guns and bought politicians—led the repeal of the Glass-Steagall Act. They needed all of 55 minutes at an April 2004 meeting to convince the SEC to ease regulatory requirements so they could take on vastly larger amounts of debt. Giant mortgage lenders like Countrywide Financial managed to have themselves placed under the lax supervision of the Office of Thrift Supervision, funded by the regulated banks themselves. The quasi-federal Fannie Mae and Freddie Mac spent millions convincing Congress to ease their capital reserve requirements. And when all this came home to roost in 2008, the very same financial institutions that had done so much to create the crisis received the vast preponderance of the funds and credits in the various

16

bailout programs that followed. Indeed, two of the 26 executives who received more compensation in 2011 than their firms paid in taxes were CEOs of financial enterprises that are alive today solely because taxpayer funding kept them that way: AIG and Citigroup.[25]

And the story—and capture—doesn't stop there. The finance sector has pushed back successfully against the most meaningful parts of the Dodd-Frank reforms, and it has been the leading advocate of the various programs for internationalization of commerce, which has permitted the proliferation of "off shore" arbitrage sites.[26]

- *Critically, CEOs have also captured the terms of debate about what it means to be a good corporate citizen.*

More than a half century ago, Frank W. Abrams, then chairman of Standard Oil of New Jersey, wrote that "The job of management is to maintain an equitable and working balance among the claims of the various directly affected interest groups," which he defined as "stockholders, employees, customers and the public at large." Today, that sort of stakeholder capitalism sounds quaint as buggy whips.

So, too, does the idea of a corporation as a kind of public private utility, to be managed for the public good. General Electric board chairman Owen Young spoke eloquently on that subject at the 1927 dedication of the Baker Library, at the Harvard Business School. One wonders if today's crop of MBAs from the leading business schools could even begin to comprehend the message Young was delivering.

The job of modern management is to maximize profits at virtually all costs, but with no concomitant obligation to distribute those profits equitably among all contributing parties. As Hedrick Smith has pointed out, American productivity increased by over 80 percent from 1973 to 2011, while average wages grew by only 4.2 percent and wages-plus-benefits by only 10 percent. Prior to the 2007-08 financial crisis, corporate profits represented the largest share of national income since the start of World War II, while the share of those profits going to wages and salaries had sunk to the lowest level since the Great Crash of 1929. Now, corporate profits are soaring once again. CEO compensation, as we've seen, is happily rocketing through the

17

stratosphere, and middle class incomes remain stagnant and new job hiring anemic.[27]

This is the true "personhood" that corporations have assumed: profit-crazed humanoids. Like Mary Shelley's Frankenstein, they mimic human form without ever achieving true humanity, in all its complex dimensionality, including that most human of all attributes, a moral conscience. And this is what corporate citizenship has come down to in our time. Decisions that once might have been subject to moral consideration—the danger of polluting waterways—for example, are now subject to cost-benefit analyses. All workers today, in corporate calculations, have price points beyond which they (and their families, their health care, their pensions, etc.) are expendable. And the true horror is that we don't even think much about it anymore.

Leading economists fall in line. Prominent business theorists tell us that this is what life is like in the new, fiercely global economy—despite the fact that nations like Germany manage to compete quite robustly while still respecting the old social contract between employers and employees. For the most part, the chattering classes blithely accept that all these canceled pension plans were bonus add-ons sadly lost to the new economic realities, not deferred compensation never to be recovered.

For the most part, too, it's political death to mention the continuing plight of the urban poor, while the poor themselves offer rich pickings for slumlords (the poor have to live somewhere, and the federal Earned Income Tax Credit is commonly used to pay off back rent), the payday lending industry (a $7 billion business these days, with more outlets than McDonald's), and subprime lenders (at least in the Good Old Days, before that bubble broke). Meanwhile, for very good reason, the real estate, finance, and insurance industries remain the largest combined sector donors to *both* the Democratic and Republican parties. [28]

And when companies like Bain Consulting reap untold millions in profits by using borrowed capital to buy companies, then sucking them dry, leaving the remains for bankruptcy referees to sort through, and stashing vast profits in offshore tax havens, we celebrate the wonders of "creative destruction" and nominate one of its primary architects for the highest office in the land.

Any Somali pirate would approve, but in one sense at least, piracy is the point here. We can admire the pluck, the sheer audacity of those who prowl the ancient waters of the Mediterranean and Red Sea in Zodiac boats, but the various facets of capture I have been describing here are not victimless acts. People—those on whom solemn obligations are off-loaded in the name of purifying profit—suffer. As we'll see in Chapter 6, profitability suffers, too, oddly by too much attention upon it. A society that values share price and market cap above all else suffers as well, but what suffers most of all are those who allow this to happen.

"Power tends to corrupt," as the famous old adage from Lord Acton contends, "and absolute power corrupts absolutely." But inaction in the face of rogue power corrupts even worse and absolute inaction, or an absolute unwillingness to confront the corporation as it is, corrupts most of all. Financial markets today are both increasingly volatile and too often massively distorted for the benefit of the very few. Empowered by the Supreme Court and unrestrained by compliant boards, CEOs have been granted license to employ our assets, investments, pension funds, etc., against our own best interests. Not all CEOs take advantage, of course, but enough do that the entire infrastructure of democratic capitalism can well be said to hang in the balance. Simply put, this is an unsustainable situation.

All of which leads to an obvious question: *How did we get here?*

****

2.
Corporations Without Owners

One small paragraph in Justice Anthony Kennedy's 57-page majority opinion in the 2010 *Citizens United* case nicely enshrines the ideal of corporate ownership as a kind of capitalist democracy:

> *With the advent of the Internet, prompt disclosure of expenditures can provide shareholders and citizens with the information needed to hold corporations and elected officials accountable for their positions and supporters. Shareholders can determine whether their corporation's political speech advances the corporation's interest in making profits, and citizens can see whether elected officials are "in the pocket" of so-called moneyed interests.*

Yes, corporations through their political donations might sometimes stray from the best economic interests of their shareholders, just as elected officials sometimes stray from the best interests of the people they represent. And, yes, corporations might also refuse to divulge to shareholders to whom and to what causes those donations are made, and indeed be legally protected from doing so. But empowered by the information superhighway, shareholders have it within their power, Justice Kennedy tells us, to uncover this data, tug hard on the reins if need be, and bring management back to the straight and narrow.

Proxy voting statements feed much the same ideal. They are rife these days with the language of corporate democracy: "independent" directors representing shareholder interest, "say on pay" votes on executive compensation, "majority voting" for directors, and on and on.

A host of data further supports the impression that corporations are entering an almost Periclean era of enlightened ownership/ management characterized by newly assertive boards and newly collaborative CEOs. The number of S&P 500 companies with separate CEOs and board chairs has risen from 16 percent in 1998 to 39 percent in 2011. Meanwhile, independent "lead" or "presiding" directors, virtually unknown a decade ago, can now be found at nearly two in five S&P 500s. Directors also have more skin in the game: 77 percent of those at S&P 500 companies have at least part of their fees for service tied up in equity. It's no longer just a matter of showing up for quarterly board meetings and pocketing a fat retainer. Engagement counts, in the wallet where it matters. [29]

All in all, it's an impressive record . . . until one bothers to look under the tent flap. Take the phrase "majority voting." Given that virtually all director slates are uncontested—that is, the number of directors offered up for voting equals the number of seats on the board—requiring that directors be seated only if they win a majority of all votes cast makes compelling sense. Otherwise, a director could win a seat with a single vote, perhaps (assuming he's a shareholder in the company) his own vote.

The trouble lies with execution, not theory, as the Council for Institutional Investors points out:

> *Companies that have embraced majority voting for directors generally allow their boards to second-guess shareowners when an incumbent director falls short of majority support in an uncontested election. They do so through policies that require the director to tender his/her resignation but give the board broad discretion in deciding whether to accept it.*
>
> *As a result, directors are losing elections but not their board seats. In 2011, more than 40 directors at 30-plus companies in the Russell 3000 index failed to win a majority of the votes cast, yet nearly all kept their board seats, according to ISS (Institutional Shareholder Services). In 2010, 106 "failed" directors at 59 companies remained on boards.* [30]

In short, "majority voting" has far more to do with the whim of a majority of directors and, critically, the CEO than it does with the expressed desires of a majority of shareholders—hardly Democracy in Motion. And so it goes, to a greater or lesser degree, through the entire panoply of (presumed) shareowner empowerment. On paper, great. In practice, too often an exercise in Orwellian doublespeak in which the language itself comes largely to mean its opposite. Some examples:

- *Board election.*

When tin-pot dictators run uncontested for office, station thugs at the polls, and declare themselves the people's choice with 99.999 percent of the vote (allowing for error), we know the language of democracy is being gamed. When corporations hold similar elections for their boards of directors, most of us barely blink. And yet, really, what is the difference?

No one would describe the reality of how individuals accede to board membership as an *election* in the sense that the word is commonly understood by political scientists, or even the public at large. For starters, no individual appears on the company's proxy statement for election to a vacancy except with the approval of the chief executive officer and the incumbent board members. Only in the rarest instance, as noted earlier, are there more individuals enumerated on the proxy card than there are vacancies. And if you doubt white-collar thugs are guarding the polls, I invite you to try introducing onto the ballot a name not sanctioned by those in complete control of the nominating process. In 1991, I nominated myself for a position as director of Sears Roebuck, a prospect apparently so horrific to the management that the company spent an acknowledged $20 million of shareholder equity to defeat me. That was more than two decades ago, of course. Today, the thugs that guard the corporate polls operate with the full weight of the U.S. Court of Appeals for the District of Columbia behind them, as we'll see shortly.

True, director slates *are* sometimes challenged in their entirety by rival groups willing to produce separate proxy materials, engage professional proxy solicitors, hire on the requisite investment bankers and the like—expenses that can easily reach to $3 million or more.

But how successful are such efforts? To find out, Harvard Law School Professor Lucian A. Bebchuk surveyed the 303 contested solicitations that occurred over the ten years 1996 to 2005, roughly 30 a year, itself an indication of just how rare such challenges are. Of those 303 contests, 88 focused on the takeover or sale of the company, 74 did not involve the election of directors, and 23 had to do with opening or restructuring a closed-end fund. That left 118 contests that focused specifically on an alternative team for governing the company, and of those, 45 were ultimately successful, or 4.5 challenges a year over a ten-year span that included the tumultuous tech-bubble burst of 2001-2002, the implosion of Enron, the collapse of WorldCom, and much more that should have spurred corporate owners to action. Again, hardly Democracy in Motion. [31]

- *Director*

If *election* is a ritual mostly without meaning in the modern corporate world, *director* is a position almost entirely without substance. What do directors direct? One could cite a number of areas in which directors seemingly have sway: issues of corporate strategy, CEO succession, mergers and acquisitions, and the like. Directors do, after all, often bring a wealth of experience to the job. But the utter failure of boards as a whole to control in the least executive compensation argues that in the area where directors should exercise the most authority, they exercise the least. If the principals either cannot or will not manage their agent's draw on the corporate treasury, what cause do we have to assume that they exercise effective accountability—i.e., direction—in any other area either?

More than thirty years ago, Peter Drucker questioned whether the current standard of board functioning is so unsatisfactory as to require structural change: "Whenever an institution malfunctions as consistently as boards of directors have in nearly every major fiasco of the last forty or fifty years, it is futile to blame men. It is the institution that malfunctions." [32] The fiascos continue unabated.

- *Independence*

Here we come upon a sort of semantic Potemkin village. When

corporations speak of "independent" directors, they have in mind a legal and regulatory standard: Such directors cannot be in the employ of the body they oversee or have other contractual arrangements — excepting, of course, retainers for service on the board and attendant equity arrangements.

Such legal *independence*, though, has little to do with the broader meaning of the word itself, especially when applied to corporate boards. Directors may or may not be independent-minded, but under the current system, in which boards of directors are essentially self-perpetuating, it goes beyond credulity to think that any individual board member could be considered to be "independent" of the board as a whole and the CEO.

Directors want their jobs — for the prestige, the power, the financial gain. And the bigger the corporation, the more coveted the position. They also want to retain the position once secured. In the circle in which such people travel, to be removed as a director is a horrible stain, not just professionally but personally. Thus, those chosen and endorsed by management inherently have a conflict of interest. They cannot be entrusted with auditing and compensating management, among other duties, without destroying the legitimacy of the process.

The SEC clearly recognized this in August 2010 when it adopted new rules requiring corporations to include in their proxy materials board nominees put forward by significant, long-term shareholders, here defined as holding at least 3 percent of a company's shares continuously for at least three years.

"As a matter of fairness and accountability, long-term significant shareholders should have a means of nominating candidates to the boards of the companies that they own," SEC Chairman Mary L. Schapiro said in announcing the new rules. "Nominating a director candidate is not the same as electing a candidate to the board. I have great faith in the collective wisdom of shareholders to determine which competing candidates will best fulfill the responsibilities of serving as a director. The critical point is that shareholders have the ability to make this choice."[33]

Even this modest nod to meaningful independence, though, proved abhorrent to the corporation-dominated U.S. Chamber of Commerce and the CEO-dominated Business Roundtable. In an April 2011 filing with the U.S. Court of Appeals for the District of Columbia, lawyers for both petitioners argued that, under the new SEC rules, "special interest investors would use proxy access as leverage to obtain concessions from companies; as a 'soap-box' to voice disagreements with company policy; and to seek the election of candidates favorable to the special interests of labor unions or the political officials in charge of government pension funds."

In other words, the potential inconveniences of corporate democracy take precedence over its realization and practice, just as the potential costs to those already in power take precedence over the heady costs to be incurred by those who might seek to remove them or alter in the slightest their composition. In the end, the appeals courts apparently agreed. A three-judge panel ruled unanimously that the SEC had overstepped its bounds, and a majority of SEC commissioners declined to pursue the cause further.[34]

- *Shareholder rights*

Another entry in the Orwellian dictionary of corporate democracy, shareholder "rights" are almost solely a function of state law, which has been so skewed by corporate lobbying that shareholders in effect have no meaningful rights at all.

Consider the "right to remove a director" under Delaware law. Yes, we are solemnly told, Delaware law provides that you can remove a director, but you can call a meeting at which to accomplish this sometimes needed act only if you are the CEO or a plurality of the directors—yet another reason why so many companies incorporate in Delaware.

Or consider the soliciting of proxies, just about the sole shareholder "right" that falls under federal jurisdiction—the SEC, in this case—since it involves interstate commerce. Shareholders are, indeed, free as birds in the sky and fish in the sea to propose whatever they like, but the SEC alone, and all but immunized from appeal, determines which proposals it will force management to include on the proxy, thus setting itself up as censor in chief of permitted communication from shareholders to their fellows via the free medium of the annual meeting proxy.

As intolerable as that is, the situation is made even worse by the utter capriciousness with which these federal censors wield their power. For ten consecutive years, I filed virtually identical proposals with the SEC that would have called for a shareholder vote on whether ExxonMobil should separate the positions of CEO and Chairman of the Board. In three of those years, the SEC threw my proposal out. Seven years, for no apparent reason, my proposal made it to corporate headquarters. Even then, I had to shell out $50,000 per "success" to a New Jersey lawyer willing to counter Exxon's own attempt to quash the proposal, and still, after all that, there was absolutely nothing obligatory about the proxy I submitted. It was precatory—a formal request; nothing more was allowed. A 100 percent vote in its favor would do nothing to compel the ExxonMobil board to do a single thing.[35]

Thus, for example, when Citigroup shareholders rejected the company's proposed executive compensation package at its April 2012 annual meeting by a 55 to 45 percent vote, CEO Vikram Pandit could blandly sidestep the results with assurances that the board would take the "say on pay" vote into account. (Pandit, to be sure, was forced into retirement half a year later, but for gross incompetence, not for dismissing a vote margin that has been exceeded in only 10 of the 56 presidential elections in which the popular vote was tallied.)[36]

"If the SEC approves of the material, it cannot be important," an old maxim goes. "If it is important, the SEC will throw it out." But either way and whatever the subject at hand—executive pay, environmental effects, political contributions, separation of CEO and board chair—this is a shareholder "right" that amounts to little more than a meaningless proposal expensively placed on a ballot, with no impact however the resulting vote falls.

Thus, with every good (if stunningly naïve) intention, stands Supreme Court Justice Anthony Kennedy's ultimate line of shareowner defense against the corporate abuse of the political process that would otherwise seem inherent in the *Citizens United* decision: majority voting that doesn't count; elections that are uncontested; directors who don't direct in the most consequential matters; independence that is alternately an oxymoron, a laughingstock, and a chimera; and shareholder rights that don't pass the most elementary tests of a true democracy.[37]

This is not what the founders of corporations or the early framers of corporate law had in mind.

A Very Short History of the Corporation

1.   Corporations are rooted in the principle of ownership, the moral nature of which has been confounding humans since prehistory. The early Christian Church thought ownership the root of most evil. Aristotle, by contrast, believed that ownership both taught and encouraged public responsibility. Adam Smith famously reconciled the two points of view when he wrote, in *The Wealth of Nations*, that even if a businessman "intends only his own gain, he is . . . led by an invisible hand to promote an end which is not his intention." Indeed, Smith believed that, "by pursuing his own interest, he frequently promotes that of society more effectively than when he really intends to promote it."[38]

2.   The first corporate-like entities were towns, monastic orders, and universities that emerged in the Middle Ages, collectively organized to counter the power of monarchs, later extended to centralized governments generally. The City of London—the roughly one-square mile of old London that now houses a global financial hub—was chartered by William the Conqueror in 1075. The University of Paris, commonly called the Sorbonne, was granted a "diploma" by King Phillip II in 1200 "for the security of the scholars of Paris." In both cases, assets were held by the entity itself, not by a collection of partners, assuring perpetuity.

3.   The British East India Company, founded on the last day of 1600, and the Dutch East India Company established in 1602 are

generally considered the first modern corporations. Jointly owned by their shareholders, the companies operated under royal charters that granted them extraordinary powers in the expectation of economic gain that would benefit both crown and country. The pattern of private-state economic cooperation via corporations thus became engrained in Western economic culture, as did the risks.

4.   The success of both the Dutch and British East India companies spawned a host of unlicensed stock-issuing imitators. Bubble followed bubble as speculation grew until the spectacular collapse of the South Sea Company bubble in August 1720 bankrupted thousands of Englishmen, including multiple members of the British Parliament. To prevent a recurrence (and protect Members of Parliament from their own worst instincts), Parliament that autumn passed the Bubbles Act, requiring all companies to obtain a certificate of incorporation before issuing stock, and the long and sometimes confusing cloak of bureaucracy first cast its shadow over corporations.

5.   In his *Commentaries on the Laws of England* (1765-69), the great English jurist Sir William Blackstone listed the five powers "inseparably incident to every corporation" as follows:

- "To have perpetual succession. This is the very end of its incorporation: for there cannot be a succession forever without an incorporation."

- "To sue or be sued, implead or be impleaded, grant or receive, by its corporate name, and do all other acts as natural persons may."

- "To purchase lands and hold them, for the benefit of themselves and their successors: which two are consequential of the former."

- "To have a common seal . . . . For, though private members may express their private consents to any act, by words, or by signing their names; yet this does not bind the corporation: It is the fixing of the seal, and that only, which unites the several assents of the individuals, who compose the community, and makes one joint assent of the whole."

- "To make by-laws or private statutes for the better government of the corporation; which are binding upon themselves, unless contrary to the laws of the land, and then they are void. This is also included by law in the very act of incorporation: for as natural reason is given to the natural body for the governing it, so by-laws or statutes are a sort of political reason to govern the body politic."[39]

6.   In the wake of the American Revolution, Blackstone's legal understanding of the fundamental nature of the corporation was imported to the New World, but with significantly different historical and evolutionary pulls. An early flirtation with granting Congress the power to charter corporations ended when Andrew Jackson put the Bank of the United States out of business and such authority devolved to the states. Corporate ownership also became far more broadly based in the United States than in any other Western nation, and the American government, unlike its European counterparts, sat mostly on the sidelines as private interests developed critical national industries.

7.   Granted such near autonomy, U.S. corporations became the greatest wealth-producing entities the world has ever known, and Americans have been arguing about them ever since—their good, their bad and ugly; the appropriate regulatory environment surrounding them; and (the intersection where Blackstone and *Citizens United* collide) just how "natural" a person a soulless corporation can be and what rights and powers are appropriate to its peculiar legal form.[40]

Concentrated Wealth, Spreading Corruption, and Political Domination

Early concerns about corporations tended to center on the concentration of wealth and the potential for such wealth to corrupt the political process and, in the extreme, subvert the nation itself. Abraham Lincoln had been elected to a second term as president only a few weeks earlier—the surrender at Appomattox was still nearly five months away—when he wrote to Col. William Elkins on November 21, 1864, of a crisis approaching in the near future "that unnerves me and causes me to tremble for the safety of my country":

30

*As a result of the war, corporations have been enthroned and
an era of corruption in high places will follow, and the money
power of the country will endeavor to prolong its reign by
working upon the prejudices of the people until all wealth is
aggregated in a few hands and the Republic is destroyed. I
feel at this moment more anxiety for the safety of my country
than ever before, even in the midst of war. God grant that my
suspicions may prove groundless.*

Theodore Roosevelt sounded much the same theme—and used
some of the same imagery—in an August 1912 speech during his
presidential campaign as the candidate of the Progressive Party:
"Behind the ostensible government sits enthroned an invisible
government owing no allegiance and acknowledging no responsibility
to the people. To destroy this invisible government, to befoul the
unholy alliance between corrupt business and corrupt politics is the
first task of the statesmanship of the day."[41]

But Teddy Roosevelt had a more nuanced view of the corporation
than his "trust-busting" reputation might suggest. In his 1913
autobiography, the aging Rough Rider drew a bright line between
corporate practices that harm and those that serve the common good.
The former, he wrote, are "a conspiracy against the public welfare,"
while the latter "promote abundance by cheapening the cost of
living so as to improve conditions everywhere throughout the whole
community."[42]

The dual nature of corporations—able business and legal
mechanisms, cash machines that threaten the integrity of the political
process; raisers of mankind, conspiracies against the common good—
was still on display two decades later when, in the midst of the
Great Depression, Supreme Court Justice Louis Brandeis issued his
dissenting opinion in *Liggett Co. v. Lee*: "Through size, corporations,
once merely an efficient tool employed by individuals in the conduct
of private business, have become an institution—an institution which
has brought such concentration of economic power that so-called
private corporations are sometimes able to dominate the state."[43]

Brandeis, though, drilled deeper. It wasn't just the concentrated wealth corporations represented that was at issue. It was their ownership, or more accurately, the reality that ownership was rapidly becoming divorced from control. In theory, millions of shareholders owned U.S. Steel or Pennsylvania Railroad or the other corporate behemoths of the day. This, after all, is what corporations had been created to bring into existence: pooled resources, shared rewards and risks, mutual purpose and authority, institutional perpetuity, and out of all that, profit. In reality, the more successful corporations became at creating the last of those goals—profit—the more people wanted in on the game; and the more "owners" each company had, the less meaningful became each ownership stake.

In Brandeis's words:

The typical business corporation of the last century, owned by a small group of individuals, managed by their owners, and limited in size by their private wealth, is being supplanted by huge concerns in which the lives of tens of hundreds of thousands of employees and the property of tens of hundreds of thousands of investors are subjected, through the corporate mechanism, to the control of a few men. Ownership has been separated from control; and this separation has removed many of the checks which formerly operated to curb the misuse of wealth and power. And, as ownership of the shares is becoming continually more dispersed, the power which formerly accompanied ownership is becoming increasingly concentrated in the hands of a few.

Nothing in the eighty years since has served to alter that picture for the better or diminish Brandeis's inherent warning. Indeed, a host of forces have worked in exactly the opposite direction, not merely to further separate ownership and control but to enshrine the division.[44]

Disappearing Owners

Brandeis's dissent in *Liggett v. Lee* was handed down in 1933. The year before saw the publication of *The Modern Corporation and Private Property*, by Adolph A. Berle with Gardiner Means—perhaps the most influential book ever written on the subject of corporate governance. (There's nothing like a Great Depression to focus attention on corporate matters, and nothing like good old-fashioned brains either. Berle entered Harvard College at age fourteen, earned his undergraduate and master's degrees, and then graduated from Harvard Law School at age twenty-one.)

Among Berle's many trenchant observations was the fact that what corporate shareholders possess is not ownership of property, in the sense commonly understood. The owner of industrial wealth is left with a mere symbol of ownership, while the power, the responsibility, and the substance—integral parts of ownership in the past—are transferred to a separate group in whose hands lies control. As Berle puts it, "It has often been said that the owner of a *horse* is responsible. If the *horse lives* he must feed it. If the *horse dies* he must bury it. No such responsibility attaches to a share of stock."[45]

Therein lies the foundational problem with corporate ownership: It's loosey-goosey to begin with. One share of a million outstanding in a corporation entitles the holder to one-millionth of the pot if the enterprise liquidates and dissolves, but does it entitle the shareholder to one-millionth of whatever good or service is being produced and offered for sale? Does it obligate the holder to one-millionth of the responsibility if the production of that good or service pollutes a waterway, restrains trade, or impinges on a patent? Does it give the shareholder one-millionth of the say in mergers and acquisitions, selection and compensation of senior management, and the disbursal of political contributions?

In theory, again, yes. If there were such a thing as corporate democracy, then all shareholders in a particular corporation would be mutually obligated, entitled, and empowered. But as Charles Lindbloom writes in *Politics and Markets*, "The large private corporation fits oddly into democratic theory and vision. Indeed, it does not fit."[46] And so, we're left with the reality of shareholder ownership, that it is structurally weak and tenuous at best when it comes to exercising any effective control over the entity shareholders own. In Adolph Berle's words from eight decades ago, "The dissolution of the atom of property destroys the very foundation on which the economic order of the past three centuries has rested."[47]

Add to that three powerful growth trends in recent decades, and the widening gap between ownership and control becomes far more understandable.

- *Scale*

In 1896, when General Electric became one of the original twelve companies included in the Dow Jones Industrial Average, its relatively few shareholders felt a clear sense of co-ownership with founder Thomas Edison. Today, GE has 10.6 billion shares of common stock outstanding — one-and-a-half shares for every man, woman, and child alive on the planet. Obviously, shareholders are infinitely more condensed than that. The Vanguard Group alone owns some 457 million shares. But when there are literally millions of "owners" of the largest companies such as GE, there is virtually no rational incentive for a single shareholder to be active in his, her, or its ownership.[48]

Scale also applies to volume. On the opening trading day of 1962, a little over 2 million shares of GE changed hands. A half century later, on the opening day of 2012, GE's trading volume hit 58.7 million shares — a 29-fold increase during a 50-year span when the global population increased by less than two-and-a-half fold. Given round-the-world, round-the-clock, round-the-year trading — more than 100 percent of outstanding shares in all companies "turn over" in any given year — there is never a single instance in time when GE's ownership is not in flux, one might even say chaotic transition.[49]

Nor, of course, do most of those with an ownership stake in GE even know they have one. That gets us to the second trend driving a wedge between owners and control.

- *Algorithms & Index Funds*

There's a split here, one of those forks in the road in which both choices arrive essentially at the same destination.

In the spring of 2010, Dow Jones launched a new service called

Lexicon, which sends out real-time financial news in a constant stream to professional investors, many of whom are machines, not human beings. To be more exact, the machine-investors are algorithms, basically lines of code that search the financial data stream for information that can trigger an instantaneous stock purchase or sale.

As Felix Salmon and Jon Stokes described the process in a December 2010 article for *Wired*, "Lexicon packages the news in a way that its robo-clients can understand. It scans every Dow Jones story in real time, looking for textual clues that might indicate how investors should feel about a stock. It then sends that information in machine-readable form to its algorithmic subscribers, which can parse it further, using the resulting data to inform their own investing decisions. Lexicon has helped automate the process of reading the news, drawing insight from it, and using that information to buy or sell a stock. The machines aren't there just to crunch numbers anymore; they're now making the decisions."[50]

As much as half of institutional ownership is now held pursuant to mathematical formulae, sometimes with disastrous results; recall the 45-minute algorithm "glitch" in the summer of 2012 that cost Knight Capital $440 million in trading losses.[51] But even when algorithms perform as advertised, they negate the involvement of human reason in the selection of particular company shares.

Indexing has the same effect, from an opposite direction. Of the nearly 450 million shares of GE that the Vanguard Group owns, fully 129 million are held in the Vanguard Total Stock Market Index Fund, another 94.5 million in the Vanguard 500 Index Fund, and 92 million in its Institutional Index Fund. That's 315 million shares in those three funds alone—over 3 percent of total outstanding common stock in GE—that exists in a kind of financial suspended animation for much of the year.[52]

It's not only that owners can't do much about ownership shares that have been intentionally removed from their control; algorithms and indexing also both have the practical effect of making shareholders indifferent to their stakes in the enterprises of which they are the titular owners.

- *Trustee Ownership*

Today, more than 70 percent of all publicly traded shares in the United States are held by trustees, legal creatures with the obligation to responsibly manage trust property "solely in the interests of, and for the exclusive benefit of, plan participants and beneficiaries."[53] One might think this alone would assure the responsible exercise of corporate ownership. Almost certainly, that 70 percent includes a majority of the voting shares of every Fortune 500 company and well beyond, and the ancient, unchanging, and inveterate requirement of trust law and practice is that the trustee is not permitted to serve its own objectives when they are in conflict with those of trust beneficiaries. How can a trustee serve the best interests of beneficiaries *without* occasionally climbing under the hood of the enterprises being relied upon to feather nests in retirement?

In fact, such has not been the case. With a few rare and honorable exceptions, trustees—including universities, foundations, and even the most enlightened corporations' pension funds—have deliberately declined to take steps as activist shareholders. There is no recorded judicial effort to enforce trust principles; there has been no action by regulators; there has not been any derivative litigation on behalf of the beneficiaries.

What this means is that mutual funds, employee benefit plans, and other relationships styled as trusts are trusts in name only and not in substance. Trustees who actively pursue the interests of their beneficiaries are in a precarious position. Good guys can't be good because they're at a competitive disadvantage. So we are left instead with layers of conflicts that all serve to widen, not narrow the gap between ownership and control. Among them:

- When trustees are a member of a conglomerate group, pursuing beneficiary interest could put them into conflict with their parent company. If the fiduciary portfolios include tradable shares from other parts of the conglomerate, how do you proceed, on behalf of the beneficiary or the parent company?

- When university or foundation trustees also represent

36

companies in the trust portfolio, which interest takes priority? Engaging such a company raises questions of comity and collegiality within the board and can make for difficult relationships.

• There has long been a rumored "Golden Rule" for pension plans set up under the federal Employment Retirement Income Security Act: "You leave my company alone, and our pension plan will leave your company alone." Whether or not this is hyperbole, there has never been a recorded case of activism by an ERISA plan. When a trustee is serving as fiduciary for a company employee benefit plan, he might well be acting contrary to the commercial interest of the sponsor company (that is, the company whose employees join the plan) by raising questions about the management of companies in the pension portfolio.

Bottom line: So long as these important institutional investors can ignore legal fiduciary obligation with respect to portfolio companies, this majority block of all voting shares is effectively sterilized. What's more, because entire categories of investors decide not to participate, they succeed in trivializing those who do.

So go the ironies of corporate ownership in our own times. Corporate governance is awash in the language of democracy: board elections, independent directors, majority voting, yet one would do better to look for democracy in some of the darker corners of the former Soviet Union than in the internal workings of virtually any major American corporation.

Meanwhile, more Americans have an ownership share in the corporate economy than ever before in human history, yet the very processes that have enabled that—massive scale, algorithmic and index trading, pension funds and trustee ownership—have so scattered ownership and diluted its significance that corporations might well be said to be less "owned," and certainly less under the control of their owners, than they ever before have been.

In the December 22, 2011, *New York Times* Chrystia Freeland reported on a panel she had recently moderated, organized by the

European Corporate Governance Institute and Columbia. The theme: the involvement of shareholders in the companies they owned. According to Freeland, the consensus of the panelists was that the United States "has created a system of capitalism without capitalists, of private sector companies whose owners have abdicated responsibility for the companies that belong to them." Certainly, that's part of the story. For a myriad of reasons, even the great and the good among institutional owners are failing to step to the plate. Nothing compels them to do so. Indeed, their self-interest—although *not* their ancient fiduciary duties—might be said to compel them in the opposite direction. [54]

Indexing and algorithms, the sheer scale of ownership and trading volume are part of the story as well. Only the most obsessive investors really know what they own, or when and how often it is traded. If shares are effectively betting slips instead of certificates of ownership, we might well ask if shareholding in the classic sense is largely a fiction—if shares now represent nothing more than the right to participate in the stock market, not in the governance of the firm issuing the certificate. If that's the case, can ownership for all practical *and* legal purposes be deemed even to exist any longer?

Underlying all this, though, is the willingness of the polity to join in the charade. Bills to require timely or even any disclosure of corporate political donations are voted down in Congress. SEC censorship assures that shareholders cannot nominate or remove a director, or even effectively communicate with one another other or with directors. No one gets paid to—or is required to—maintain accurate and accessible lists of legal and/or beneficial ownership of public companies. Nobody goes to jail because of mistakes or absences in the shareholder register. And even if all these shareholders could be easily located and contacted, nothing requires management or directors to recognize the majority or even unanimous desire of a corporation's supposedly legal owners. Thus, even shareholders who want to act like owners and can afford to do so are discouraged from battle, or driven to quixotic acts pre-doomed in almost all cases to failure.

And to the final law of the land—the Supreme Court of the United States—this is apparently just the way things should be. Back in 1978, in his majority opinion in *First National Bank of Boston v. Bellotti*, Justice Lewis Powell confidently asserted that there is little evidence of corporate abuse that cannot be corrected by shareholders "through the procedures of corporate democracy." Now along comes Justice Anthony Kennedy, citing *Bellotti* in his *Citizens United* decision as he confidently asserts that "the procedures of corporate democracy . . . can be more effective today because modern technology makes disclosures rapid and informative."[55] Only one thing is missing: the "corporate democracy" both justices rely on.

> *Question: If owners no longer control corporations, who does?*

****

3.
Manager-Kings

In the mid-1980s, investigative reporter and Kennedy assassination conspiracy theorist Edward Jay Epstein wrote a book called *Who Owns the Corporation: Management vs. Shareholders.* The accelerated atomization of ownership through mutual funds and institutional holdings was well underway, driving the transfer of control over "most of America's productive capital from its legal owners to the hands of management groups." Projecting this trend forward, Epstein envisioned a dark world in which, "Executives in control could, like Armand Hammer, the chairman of Occidental Petroleum, legally use corporate revenue to buy art, sponsor peace festivals, build international trade centers in Communist countries, make political contributions, and have private airliners at their disposal."[56]

Nearly thirty years into the future, the question begs asking: If Epstein was truly prescient, how would CEOs act today?

They Would Use Boards to Fortify Their Positions, with Little Regard for Shareholder Return.

Have they? In a word, yes.

Any number of prominent instances could be cited, from Countrywide's Angelo Mozilo to ExxonMobil's Lee Raymond, Pfizer's Henry McKinnell, Fannie Mae's Frank Raines, and well beyond. But to see how the game is played by a true master, consider the case of Sandy Weill, the former head of Citigroup. After three decades in banking and finance, Weill engineered the 1998 merger of Citicorp with Travelers Group. Technically, the merger was in violation of the Banking Act of 1933, better known as the Glass-Steagall Act, but Weill nonetheless tipped off President Bill Clinton to the impending marriage, correctly anticipating that Glass-Steagall would soon disappear.

The original merger agreement called for Weill and Travelers CEO John Reed to split the top spot at the new Citigroup conglomerate, but Weill was not one to share power gladly, or to tolerate pretenders to the throne. Just a month after the merger, he forced out his long-time right-hand man Jamie Dimon, widely considered to be a superior manager to Weill. (And indeed, Dimon would go on to become the very public CEO of JP Morgan.) A little over a year later, in early 2000, Weill secured the top spot for himself, ousting Reed after an extended power struggle.[57]

In 2002, Jack Grubman, a former star analyst for Citigroup's Salomon Smith Barney unit, explained how Weill had drafted him into this internal battle. With Weill's encouragement, Grubman had boosted AT&T's share rating from a long-standing "neutral" to a "buy." That was sufficient to secure the loyalty of AT&T's CEO, C. Michael Armstrong, who also was sitting on Citigroup's board of directors. Weill meanwhile rewarded Grubman for his cooperation by securing admission for Grubman's twin daughters and son to the highly coveted pre-school at New York's 92nd Street Y. The Citigroup Foundation subsequently gifted the 92nd Street Y with a $1 million donation. By then, Weill was thoroughly in control of the foundation's disbursements.[58]

Grubman, of course, would go on to be disgraced for such activities. Once the highest paid analyst on Wall Street, he was banned for life from the financial industry by the SEC in April 2003. No such stigma had ever been allowed to taint the reputation of Robert Rubin, the former Goldman Sachs co-chairman and Bill Clinton's Treasury secretary when Glass-Steagall was superannuated. But Rubin, who sat on Citigroup's board when Reed got cut off at the knees, was for all practical purposes as compromised as AT&T's Armstrong.

Weill had wooed the former Goldman Sachs co-chairman into dual service on the Citigroup board and as the company's "senior counselor" with a staggeringly large compensation package, estimated to total somewhere around $125 million, yet as the *Wall Street Journal* reported, Rubin's responsibilities remained "murky"—other than providing luster for a board that was "little more than a rubber stamp" during an era in which "Weill reigned supreme."[59]

Rubin and Armstrong were still Citigroup directors in 2003 when Weill stepped down as CEO, while retaining his position as Chairman of the Board. To replace Weill, the board approved his hand-picked successor, Charles Prince. Prince was notable for his loyalty to Weill— he had been his personal lawyer—and Weill could never have enough lawyers around him. He kept on retainer, at Citi's expense, just about every major law firm in Manhattan, which had the happy effect (along with Rubin's rented reputation) of virtually insulating Weill against lawsuits, given the difficulty of finding a firm capable of bringing such a lawsuit that wouldn't be caught in a conflict of interest with an existing client.

Yet, as useful as Charles Prince was for Weill's personal legal protection, he had absolutely no experience running a bank, let alone one of world's largest, and the inexperience would quickly prove telling. During Prince's four years at the helm, Citigroup shareholders lost $64 billion in market capitalization. When he was finally let go, in 2007, Weill publicly repudiated his protégé while also helping arrange a well-feathered exit: a bonus of $12.5 million, a $1.7 million pension, and an office, car, and driver for up to five years. The executive power then passed very briefly to Weill's $125 million bonus baby, Bob Rubin. After a little over a month in office, Rubin handed the duties over to Win Bischoff.[60]

By then, Weill was gone as board chair—he resigned in 2006— but Citigroup's tradition of compliant directors, neglectful governance, and plunging shareholder equity lived on. In 2008, when Citigroup almost tanked completely, its board included three CEOs whose companies had on average lost 70 percent of value during the height of the financial meltdown: Alain Belda of Alcoa, Xerox's Anne Mulcahy, and Dow Chemical's Andrew Liveris. [61]

Four years later, when Weill famously told CNBC's "Squawk

43

Box" that repealing Glass-Steagall had been a mistake and that behemoth, largely unregulated banks should be broken up, Citigroup was prime example number one.[62] The monstrous, largely unregulated bank Weill created by leading the charge to smash Glass-Steagall had traded at above $400 a share back in 2000, adjusted for dividends and splits. By the time he recanted on CNBC's "Squawk Box," in July 2012, Citigroup had been wallowing in the $25 a share range for three years. Weill himself, though, was nicely insulated from the pain. Seven months earlier, he had sold his Manhattan apartment for a reported $88 million. This is Rule No. 1 of the Thoroughly Modern CEO: Never take the hit yourself.[63]

CEOs Would Also Divorce Their Own Compensation from the Rest of the Workforce and from Any Meaningful Performance and Value Standards.

In his 2005 book *The Battle for the Soul of Capitalism*, Jack Bogle, the founder of the Vanguard funds, took note of the asymmetric growth in modern times of pay for CEOs versus the vast bulk of the American workforce. "In 1980 the compensation of the average chief executive office was 42 times that of the average worker; by 2004, the ratio had soared to 280 times that of the average worker." Today, the beat goes on. The gap widens, and corporate riches flow increasingly to the top.

The 2012 edition of the AFL-CIO's "Executive PayWatch" reports that CEOs at all S&P 500 companies received compensation averaging $12.94 million in 2011. Not only does this represent a 13.9 percent annual increase from 2010, in the midst of a lingering recession and high unemployment; CEOs also took home wages 380 times greater than that of a typical American, whose salaries have remained just about even with inflation for decades.[64]

At the very apex of the corporate hierarchy, the disparity grows even greater. In 1970 the average salary of the top 100 CEOs in the country was $1.5 million while the average salary of an American worker was $39,400. In 2011, the median salary for the 100 highest-paid CEOs was $14.4 million—a 960 percent increase over four decades. Meanwhile, the average American salary stood at $45,230, a 15 percent increase during the same time span, not adjusted for inflation. Another way to arrange the numbers: A little over four decades ago, the average CEO was bringing home the same compensation as 38 average workers. Today, the mean compensation received by the top 100 executives equals as much as the combined pay of 1,100 average workers.[65]

Bogle describes this widening income disparity as not only a flashpoint for populist anger, but also a "pathological mutation" from "traditional owners' capitalism to a new form, managers' capitalism." Among the symptoms of the pathology: compensation unrelated to performance or value added.

In the 1990s the idea that the financial markets could best determine executive compensation became increasingly dominant, with a large push from CEOs themselves Seen in one light, the theory makes sense. If market competition correctly prices everything from fashion accessories to IT outsourcing, why shouldn't it also accurately price CEO remuneration? Boards and compensation committees quickly embraced the idea as well, in part because it seemed efficient and rational and perhaps in larger part because by outsourcing compensation evaluation to the magic of the market, they could avoid the difficult decisions necessary in performance evaluation.

Whatever the reasons, an entire industry subset of compensation consultants soon emerged, spreadsheets in hand, but two problems remained unaddressed. The first was the natural tendency of compensation consultants to tell CEOs what they wanted to hear. As Charlie Munger once caustically commented about such consultants, "Prostitution would be a step up for them."[66]

The other problem is more directly foundational: No true market exists for CEO compensation. Instead, salaries begin at a very high level and then simply continue to rise, despite the fact that there are a consistent number of qualified CEO candidates and no increased demands or risks associated with the job. The "market," such as it is, is far more about justifying exorbitant wages than it is about setting them through the rigors of competition. As Ha-Joong Chang writes in

23 Things They Don't Tell You About Capitalism, the enormous power of the managerial classes in the U.S. made it "an illusion to think that executive pay is something whose optimal levels and structures are going to be, and should be, determined by the market."[67]

Examples are everywhere, none more egregious than those that followed the 2008 financial crisis. In a 2009 article for *The National Journal*, Gary Burtless of the Brookings Institution cites the then-current controversy over AIG's announcement that it would be paying $165 million in bonuses to executives at a company that had just performed a catastrophic belly flop. "Some of these managers contributed importantly to one of the most spectacular business failures in history," writes Burtless. "Without the credit extended by the U.S. government, their employer would already be bankrupt. Even with a huge infusion of federal credit, the shares of long-term investors in AIG are worth a tiny fraction of their value two or three years ago. It is hard to see how a sensibly written compensation schedule would give failing managers rich bonus payments after it is plain their decisions contributed to the destruction of their company." At AIG, these bonuses were no longer performance-based incentives but akin to annual door prizes for showing up.[68]

By a similar market logic, auto manufacturers might price their products not based on comfort, reliability, performance, etc., but on the number and severity of the recalls a particular model has been subject to over, say, the last two years. The more inconvenience and danger owners have been exposed to, the higher the price tag. Follow that logic to its nth extreme, and you would end up with an infinite cost for a car that never worked at all—or for an executive who never should have had a corner office. But this is a "market" with multiple puzzlers.

Consider the 2011 salaries of three CEOs, all within the health care industry. Stephen Hemsley, top dog at mammoth United Health, managed a company of over 100,000 employees that had produced average returns relative to the industry over the past six years. John Martin oversaw the 4,000-employee Gilead Sciences, which also had produced average returns during the same half dozen years. Finally, George Paz of Express Scripts headed a company of about 13,000 employees that had shown excellent returns versus the industry over the same time frame. Within their industry, the average CEO compensation at the time was about $8.9 million.[69]

So, based on this admittedly limited information for evaluation, to whom did this "market" decide to pay the most and how much did it pay? Answers: basically, all of them, and a ton of money. George Paz's take-home from Express Scripts for 2011: $51 million. Hemsley's United Health compensation: $48.8 million. Martin's reward from Gilead Sciences for managing by far the smallest of the companies and achieving only average returns: $43.2 million.

One might be tempted to assume price-fixing, at an extraordinarily gilded level—five to six times the industry median—except that the highest paid health care CEO in 2011 ran a company with half the number of employees as Hemsley's United Health and produced returns that were slightly above the industry average but well below those earned by Paz's Express Scripts. McKesson's John Hammergren earned nearly as much as all three other executives combined in 2012: $131 million—$359,000 a day, $15,000 an hour, $249 a minute, $4.16 a second. Every 93 minutes, asleep or awake, Hammergren earned the equivalent of the 2012 federal poverty guideline for a family of four.[70]

Such pay packages simply cannot be understood in terms of rational market-based decision making. They make sense only as expressions of the power of the chief executive officers involved— over the companies they run, over the boards they select, over the national narrative about what a corporate manager is worth, and critically over the reality of how a business is actually performing.

Eastman Kodak's Antonio Perez led his company into bankruptcy but, amazingly, still has a job and a salary in the millions. To earn it, Perez has been trying to convince creditors and possible future investors that Kodak will recover like Lazarus from the grave if only the company's retirees will loose their greedy grip on promised pension and health benefits.[71] (Or, in the words of Perez's statement announcing the bankruptcy filing: Kodak needs to "ensure our remaining legacy costs related to our transformation are fairly apportioned and scaled for the digital company of the size we are today.")

In the same spirit as Perez, after Nortel went under in 2009, Mike Zafirovski, the CEO who had stood at the helm as it sunk, sought a $12 million payout, equal to just about half of a company-wide pension benefits account that was already short by about $2.5 billion.[72] In a world without shame, what could be more sensible?

CEOs Would Create Smokescreens To Mask Their Plunder.

As executive compensation rocketed upwards in the 1990s, an increasing amount of it was paid in huge stock instruments. Between 1990 and 2007, the equity-based share of total compensation for senior managers rose from 20 percent up to 70 percent.[73] The announced idea was that these stock-heavy pay packages would align executive and shareholder interests by driving up the company's value. However, these options were so enormous—more in line with the rewards a high-risk entrepreneur might expect than with traditional pay norms for the temporary steward of an existing company—that they had the practical effect of watering down share value while allowing executives to continue to pay themselves unconscionable sums.

CEOs themselves seemed to realize this because they worked extra hard to assure that the options were being paid out behind an accounting smokescreen that occluded actual cost. In the early 1990s, the Financial Accounting Standards Board (FASB) reintroduced a recommendation that corporations record the fair value of options and charge this compensation against earnings. By not making such a change—which amounted to reporting employee wages as any other business does—CEOs were receiving the lion's share of these rapidly growing pay packages in what amounted to stealth compensation.

Led by the Business Roundtable, executives responded with a ferocity never before unleashed with regard to *any* public proposal. The outcome: FASB backed down, and the accounting industry, having been abandoned by its own board of standards, generally (and quickly) agreed that it was A-OK for corporations to pay out hundreds of millions in options that never appeared on a profit or loss statement— something, one hopes, they never could have learned in school.[74]

Fast forward two decades, and while the world is much different, with options not all that much has changed. Case in point: In August 2011, Democratic Senators Carl Levin of Michigan and Sherrod Brown of Ohio introduced, for the *third* time, legislation that would close the gap between the book value of stock options recorded when they are issued and the actual value of the options when they are exercised, often years later at many multiples of their original worth. As the tax code now stands, corporations can deduct this difference as "excess stock-based compensation," a term convoluted enough to hide a multitude of sins.

Citing IRS data, Levin contends that corporate deductions for excess stock-based compensation totaled billions of dollars from 2005 to 2009. Figures from the Joint Committee on Taxation suggest that the Levin-Brown Bill would raise about $25 billion over the next decade. But don't expect quick passage. The greatest beneficiary of this double-standard accounting in 2010 was Apple, which deducted $743 million in excess compensation and received, in effect, a tax subsidy of $260 million. The runner-up: Goldman Sachs, with $352 million in deductions and a tax subsidy of $123 million. And then there's Facebook. The IPO might have tanked, but all those founders and semi-founders, and near-founders rushing to exercise their options resulted in "excess compensation" of a whooping $16 billion, saving the company $5.6 billion in federal taxes and in effect passing on to other taxpayers the burden of making up the difference.

A word of warning: Don't try this at home, on your own tax return. Corporate persons are just like real persons except when they aren't.

Appropriately, though, it was Sandy Weill who took option-based compensation to a whole new level. Jeff Madrick described the process in his book *Age of Greed*. "He 'talked about reloading all the time,' said one banking client. Reloading was the term that described Weill's approach to executive compensation. If you cashed in some options, the company replaced them with an equivalent set of new options. In 2000, Weill exercised options on twenty million shares of Citicorp and received nearly eighteen million in their place."[76] In that year alone, Weill received total compensation of more than $224 million, and why shouldn't he have? He ran a huge bank, which essentially placed a personal, options-based ATM machine in his office that he could withdraw from at will, without limit.

A million monkeys at a million typewriters pecking away for a million years couldn't come up with a plot so perfect for plunder, but if anyone ever sought justification for this scheme—an unlikely occurrence during a Citi board meeting—the compensation committee could claim that it needed to "re-incentivize" the company's CEO. And Sandy Weill, who has been much imitated but never equaled, clearly needed *lots* of re-incentivization.

They Would Further Plunder the Corporate Treasury for Perks, Luxuries, and Self-Aggrandizement.

In the darkest corners of Edward Jay Epstein's fervid imagination was a world in which executives would not only determine their own compensation but also use corporate money to "buy art, sponsor peace festivals, build international trade centers in Communist countries, make political contributions, and have private airliners at their disposal."[77]

Thirty years later, peace festivals and trade centers in Communist countries seem quaint anachronisms, but the drive toward CEO self-aggrandizement—and the temptation to satisfy it with corporate assets—lives on. Epstein's fear, for example, that chief executives might "have private airliners at their disposal" has been fully realized in our own time.

Witness Expedia Chairman Barry Diller, who despite a personal net worth in the $2 billion range and a business plan that encourages shopping around for maximum value, accumulated $1.28 million in flight expenses in 2011 on the company's dime.[78] Witness also Omnicon's John Wren, who logged over $135,000 of vacation time on the company jet. Then there is, once again, Sandy Weill, who demanded a Citigroup jet to fly him *gratis* to a Mexican resort only weeks after U.S. taxpayers had shelled out $45 billion to rescue the financial institution he no longer headed—an act of self-indulgence memorably captured in the *New York Post* headline "Pigs Fly."[80] Recall, too, the virtual fleet of private jets that carried automaker CEO's to Washington back in 2008, so they could plead for $25 billion in taxpayer assistance for their struggling companies.[81]

Private flights, though, are only the beginning of the story. Liberty Global gave over $220,000 of company money in 2011 to charities personally selected by chairman Michael Fries. In turn, one of these grateful recipients responded by giving an award to Fries. The same year, WebMD Chairman Martin Wygod steered $1.6 million of his business's money to the Rose Foundation, an organization where he just happens to be a trustee.[82]

Other executives inventively pushing the envelope for extras, according to *Forbes*: Live Nation Chairman Irving Azoff, who received over $120,000 in health premiums; Las Vegas Sands Chairman Sheldon Adelson, whose company covered over $2.6 million of his personal security expenses, a sum more appropriate for someone doing business in Lagos, Nigeria, than in the heart of Nevada; Amazon's Jeff Bezos, whose personal-security tab came in at comparative steal (but still hefty) $1.6 million; and Tom Ward of SandRidge Energy, who reported getting $783,533 worth of "accounting support" from company employees last year.

For its part, insurance title company Fidelity National spent nearly half a million dollars entertaining executives at what is described as a 28,000-acre "working Montana ranch" that happens to be owned by Fidelity's Chairman, William P. Foley II. Fidelity also dropped $55,000 at wineries, restaurants, and a hotel owned by Foley, thus helping to supplement his relatively modest 2011 compensation estimated at $12.5 million.[83]

Chesapeake Energy's Aubrey K. McClendon deserves a special mention here, and perhaps in the long history of corporate abuses generally. In July 2012, *Reuters* reported that through a special Chesapeake unit known as AKM Operations—the boss's initials— company accountants, engineers, and supervisors had handled as much as $3 million of McClendon's personal work. Restaurants co-owned by McClendon were occupying buildings owned by Chesapeake. One

Chesapeake executive was responsible for handling personal land deals and oil- and gas-well transactions for the CEO. Meanwhile, Chesapeake's fleet of company jets was carrying the McClendon family on vacations. McClendon wrote off as a business expense a $108,000 family holiday trip to Amsterdam and Paris. On another occasion, nine female friends of McClendon's wife traveled to Bermuda on a Chesapeake jet at a cost of $23,000. Mrs. McClendon was not on board, but Chesapeake's shareholder-owners nonetheless picked up the tab—a bill that not one in ten million of them even knew existed until press accounts dragged into the open this wholesale raid on the company till.[84]

They Would Continue Self-Generosity Long After Service to the Corporation Had Ended.

When divorce proceedings forced Jack Welch's financial affairs into daylight back in 2003, headlines tended to focus on the fringe benefits still being provided to General Electric's iconic retired CEO: prime boxes at Yankee Stadium and Boston's Fenway Park, courtside seating at Madison Square Garden for Knicks games, use of GE's $80,000 per month Manhattan apartment, and so on. The real story, though, was the $420 million retirement package that Welch had carried away from GE—a pot of gold that had much to do with the $180 million reportedly settled on Welch's ex-wife, Jane Beasley.[85]

Welch, though, was hardly alone. A study undertaken by GMI Ratings (of which I am a founder) discovered that over the decade ending at 2010, 21 CEOs received so-called "walk-away" packages valued at more than $100 million, with a collective value of about $4 billion. Four fifths of that $4 billion came in the form of equity profits, deferred compensation, and pensions; the remaining fifth was composed of cash severance, salary, bonuses, and other perks.

As with on-the-job compensation, there was little obvious consistency or even rationality in terms of time served or results achieved. AT&T's Ed Whitacre was given $230 million to take a scamper after only two years on the job, while Viacom's Thomas Freston put in all of nine months on the job before being given $100 million to vacate it—approximately $365,000 for every arduous day in the C-Suite. Stanley O'Neal, generally credited with miserable stewardship of Merrill Lynch & Co. from 2002 to 2007, received a $161.5 million severance package not long before that ancient mothership nearly spun off into the celestial void, only to be grabbed up for pennies on the dollar by Bank of America. Then there's Eugene Isenberg, the long-serving head of Nabors Industries. When Isenberg stepped down as CEO of the company in 2011, after 24 years on the job, he automatically triggered a $100 million payout while still retaining the title of Chairman of the Board. [86]

The purpose here isn't to argue that CEOs shouldn't be rewarded in direct proportion to the rewards for shareholders. Jack Welch was in many ways a model CEO during his twenty years at the helm of GE, and GE grew robustly during Welch's reign. But Welch was also very well compensated during those two decades. In effect, GE's board, hand-picked by Welch, rewarded him twice for his services, the second time with a pension that will pay him $9 million annually as long as he lives. For GE, one could argue, that's chump change, but why then does it take divorce proceedings to drag these numbers forward to the public eye?[87]

Finally, CEOs Would Stifle Dissent by All Available Means and Wherever It Appeared

Here, inevitably, we circle back to the Supreme Court's decision in *Citizens United*, which affirmed personhood for corporations and extended its reach into the political arena at the same time CEOs were appropriating corporate personhood for their own personal gain: a perfect storm—and a grotesque imbalance between the power of manager-kings to influence our political life and what used to be the counterbalancing power of potentially competing entities.

Example One: the continuing effort, already noted, by the Business Roundtable to muzzle proxy advisory services, particularly on compensation issues, and the parallel effort by Martin Lipton of the law firm of Wachtell, Lipton, Rosen & Katz to squelch the Harvard Law School's Shareholder Rights Project, a small, clinical program focusing on basic abuses in corporate governance. When the lobbying arm representing the CEOs of many of the nation's largest companies and the most highly paid legal defender of the autocratic rights of corporate manager-kings insist on using elephant guns to kill ants, you can be certain big money is at stake and the exercise of free speech lies in the balance.[88]

Example Two, related to One: the November 2012 ethics complaint against New York State Comptroller Thomas DiNapoli filed by Chevron. Chevron's contention: that DiNapoli, whose position is elective, had received $60,000 in campaign contributions from lawyers and consultants seeking favorable settlement of environmental litigation against the oil giant brought by the Ecuadorian government. The back story is more complicated.

In his role as overseer of the New York State Common Retirement Fund (which includes $800 million in Chevron shares), DiNapoli had been among a group of 40 institutional investors with combined assets of $580 billion who wrote to Chevron, calling on it to settle the Ecuador case. That was insult enough to Chevron CEO and Chairman John Watson, who opposed settlement. Worse, Watson was simultaneously dealing with a shareholder resolution calling on the company to separate the positions of CEO and chairman. The resolution had gone down to defeat despite support from Institutional Shareholder Services (see above) and a strong (38 percent) vote in its favor, but that 38 percent had included Dutch pension fund giant PGGM, which said that the combined CEO/chairman role is "obviously compromised," and it had been accompanied by strong (though again losing) votes for investor proposals on environmental, social, and governance issues.

The ethics complaint against DiNapoli was part of Watson and Chevron's response—trumped-up nonsense dignified (if that can possibly be the word) with the imprimatur of a white-shoes New York law firm. The other part was more chilling. Attorneys for the oil company demanded all DiNapoli's documents relating to a series of shareholder resolutions on the matter going back seven years to 2005, including institutions such as the California Public Employees' Retirement System (CalPERS), Trillium Asset Management, Boston

Common Asset Management, and others.[89]

This, of course, is almost the very definition of a nuisance action, meant to exhaust often scarce resources while firing a warning shot across the bow of other organizations and administrators that might contemplate similar action. But it's also the same disproportionality that corporations and CEOs bring to all fights. The $60,000 in tainted contributions that DiNapoli is accused of receiving equals less than 1.5 percent of the $4 million that Chevron showered on the 2012 election cycle and only .8 percent of the $7 million-plus the company spent on lobbying in 2012, including salaries and bonuses for 35 lobbyists (out of 48 total) who had previously worked in the federal government. Another elephant gun, in short—another ant.[90]

Example Three: The power of CEOs, under *Citizens United*, to direct political contributions absent any consultation with shareholder-owners and with no public disclosure, while union members have the express authority to decline to have any portion of their dues used for political purposes. This puts to rout the frequently expressed argument that in *Citizens United*, the Court was simply handing corporations equivalent political rights to those already exercised by unions. Such symmetry is nowhere present.

Example Four, and a corollary of One, Two, and Three: The reality that shareholders don't have even the same rights union members do. These purported corporate "owners" have no say whatsoever over the amount of corporate assets devoted to political causes or candidates, or the causes and candidates themselves, and no way to compel disclosure before or after the fact, other than proxy voting that CEOs and their boards are free to ignore. The power of business lobbies to preserve this obscene distinction provides further evidence of the unaccountable power of manager-kings. The manager-kings themselves are providing all the evidence necessary of their willingness to use this new-found authority in chilling ways throughout their own fiefdoms.

Consider the letter David Siegel, CEO of Westgate Resorts, sent out to his 7,000 employees in advance of the 2012 presidential election:

55

"The economy doesn't currently pose a threat to your job," Siegel wrote. "What does threaten your job, however, is another four years of the same presidential administration. If any new taxes are levied on me, or my company, as our current president plans, I will have no choice but to reduce the size of this company."

Contacted by *New York Times* reporter Steven Greenhouse, Siegel explained: "There's no way I can pressure anybody. I'm not in the voting booth with them." Therein lies, perhaps, the very definition of disingenuous.

Dave Robertson, the president of Koch Industries, sent a similar letter in October 2012 to the more than 30,000 employees of Koch-owned Georgia-Pacific, attacking government subsidies for "a few favored cronies" as well as "unprecedented regulatory burdens on businesses." If the present administration were to remain in office, Robertson warned, "Many of our more than 50,000 U.S. employees and contractors may suffer the consequences, including higher gasoline prices, runaway inflation and other ills."

Like Siegel, Robertson issued the obligatory denial. "We make it clear that any decision about which candidates to support belongs solely to our employees." But in a down economy for workers many of whom are making marginal wages, the threat to life and livelihood not only constitutes a real and present danger but calls to mind an earlier, more explicitly ugly time in American history when voting rights were largely predicated on right voting.[91]

True, unions do regularly advise their rank and file how to vote, and devote enormous human resources to the effort, but at the end of day in these modern times, union power consists largely of collective jaw-boning. Corporate power is of an entire other and more immediate order, and like 100-eyed Argus, it never rests.

Witness here the continuing, post-election effort to influence final rules on the Affordable Health Care Act led by an assortment of CEOs, including Papa John's Pizza king John Schnatter. According to Schnatter, complying with the act will cost his company $5 to $8 million a year and add 10 to 14 cents to the price of a typical Papa

John's pie.

First, the numbers: *Forbes* staff writer Caleb Melby crunched them and found that even the top figure—$8 million—would amount to a .7 percent increase in expenses for a company with $1.218 billion in revenues in 2011. Proportionally, that should equal a per-pie increase of 4.6 cents, a third of what Schnatter has claimed. As for the $8 million figure, it pales in comparison to the $24 to $32 million in pizza that Papa John's gave away as part of a September 2012 promotional.[92]

Second, Schnatter: He is not likely to feel the pain personally. He owns six million-plus shares of Papa John's, roughly a quarter of the company, worth about $300 million, and lives in Louisville, Kentucky, in a 40,000-square-foot mansion with multiple swimming pools, a 22-car garage, and a private golf course.[93]

The larger point, though, is that the circumstances of Schnatter's own wealth or the accuracy—or significance—of the numbers he made such a public fuss over hardly matter. Nor does it particularly matter except in the short term that multiple Facebook sites have popped up in protest to Schnatter's stand on Obamacare or that followers of the social news site Reddit were voting 5 to 1 in favor of boycotting Papa John's within a week of the flap going at least slightly viral. Nor is it really significant for these purposes that, while Schnatter owns a quarter of his business, that is, after all, only 25 percent. As of November 2012, three institutional investors alone controlled nearly as much stock: FMR (11.6%), BlackRock (6.7%), and JP Morgan Chase (5%). Where do they stand on Obamacare? On the prospect of marginally more expensive pizza? On the parallel prospect of health care being extended to thousands of Papa John's employees, who now are without it and either depend on the public dole for their medical services or, just as likely, go without them? Who knows? These silent partners are truly that.[94]

What matters for practical and immediate purposes—for Obamacare and with so much else about our collective political and legislative life—is who controls the story, and no other group, no other entity of any kind has the resources *and*, critically, the will to repeat falsehoods and questionable assumptions time and time and time again until they assume the patina of truth and eventually unassailable assertions. No other entity also is so unencumbered by meaningful opposition within its own ranks or by any obligation to act on or even listen to dissent.

We'll get to that later, but for now, this is what it means to be a CEO in America in the second decade of the 21st century: You can do pretty much whatever you want, you have basically unlimited access to corporate resources to promote your own agenda and your own comfort, and you speak and act with the full and majestic force of your corporation behind you whatever its titular owners might believe. As Justice John Paul Stevens concludes near the end of his lengthy dissent in *Citizens United*:

> *The Court's blinkered and aphoristic approach to the First Amendment may well promote corporate power at the cost of the individual and collective self-expression the Amendment was meant to serve. It will undoubtedly cripple the ability of ordinary citizens, Congress, and the States to adopt even limited measures to protect against corporate domination of the electoral process. Americans may be forgiven if they do not feel the Court has advanced the cause of self-government today.*[95]

With a single decision, a 5-4 majority of the Supreme Court had, in effect, handed CEOs the keys to the kingdom, the legal cover to merge corporate "personhood" with their own person and the legal right to use shareholder resources to their own ends. They could now move beyond treating their corporations as personal fiefdoms and aim their sights on a much bigger target: government itself.

Question: Have they exercised this legal authority?

****

4.

Made in the U.C.A.

A beautiful mid-April day in Palm Beach. The sun is just beginning to set over Everglades Island. The help, a husband-wife team born in the Philippines and now at home on three continents, moves silently, delivering drinks and passing a platter of exquisite hors d'oeuvres.

The host studies his guests over the rim of his glass as they settle into the pleasant, pre-dinner routines. His name is a commonplace of the Washington press, a lawyer-lobbyist whose tentacles run deep into the highest echelons of government and business. But no one here is anonymous. Assembled on this veranda with the host are four CEOs of some of America's largest corporations.

The collective annual revenue of the businesses they run exceeds $1.3 trillion, a tick shy of the gross national product of Spain, a nation of 47 million people. The pay of these executives is no less impressive, an average of about $45 million annually. Add in the host and the pooled compensation of the five totals roughly $200 million, equal to the combined income of 4,000 families earning $50,000 annually, the 2011 median for American households.

One might expect that an invitation to such a gathering, among such business and legal glitterati, would arrive in gilt, on embossed stationery, perhaps delivered on a silver tray by liveried servants. But not so. Everyone knows each other. The host called. Schedules were rearranged, some hastily. Corporate jets were deployed. Everyone came. Now, the host raises his glass.

"A toast . . . but to what?" The question is rhetorical, a party game. He turns to the guest on his far left.

"Too big to fail?" Guest Number One ventures, with what in a lesser man might have been taken for a smirk. His industrial concern, one of the world's largest, would have surely gone under in 2008 without the federally administered Troubled Asset Relief Program. Happily, his salary and benefits survived undiminished as well.

"Be humble in victory," the host reminds him as he takes a sip and turns to the somewhat portly man to his immediate right.

"What are we drinking to, George?"

"The President, of course," George answers, tipping his glass with a flourish. No one on the veranda had favored the president for reelection, but these are prudent men. They hedged their bets carefully, and their host engaged the requisite number of displaced congressmen and officials from the president's first term to assure ready access to the White House, Capitol Hill, and points in between and beyond. The guiding principle is a simple one: The more things change, the more they should stay the same.

"Hail to the Chief," the host replies, with an equal tip, and moves his attention to George's left, a svelte banker with a permanent tan.

"My turn?"

"If you want to play."

"But, of course. I propose a toast to those two great retired public servants Christopher Dodd and Barney Frank."

A knowing chuckle goes around the room. The U.S. Chamber of Commerce and allied groups had spent a fortune in corporate assets, assuring that when the Dodd-Frank Wall Street Reform and Consumer Protection Act finally was signed into law, in July 2010, it would reform little meaningful and protect almost nothing.

"What could be more useful than useless regulation," the host agrees, with a modest shrug. He had been in the room when the "t's" were crossed and "i's" dotted on the final version of the legislation, long after the president had signed it into law. He nods now to the last of those being queried, the craggy-faced CEO of a global energy giant.

"Might I be parochial?"

Again, the host nods.

"Then I toast creationism."

A slight gasp of surprise sweeps across the veranda. God was much favored by the politicians who courted these men, but He was never alluded to in their own version of polite society.

The oilman continues with a slight smile. "You heard me right: creationism. The sure faith that *all* this" — he waves his arm grandly across the sky — "is pre-ordained. It's *so* much more user friendly than actual science." With that, the tension breaks, and joviality returns. Within the tight circle of top CEOs, the energy mogul has long been admired for employing shareholder assets to debunk theories related to global climate change.

The servant is already refilling glasses as attention turns to the host himself. It's his turn to play.

"And you, John?" George asks. "Would you like to propose a toast?"

"I would," he answers, raising his glass high. "Here's to capture."

Capture? The word hangs in the air, waiting explication.

"Don't you see?" the host says. "We've got it. The White House, Congress, the Supremes, the regulators — we've finally treed them all. And the intellectuals and chattering classes too. The politicians line up for our money. They advise and consent on court nominees." (Here, he can't resist a chuckle of his own.) "The regulators want to come to work for us, for you and me, when their children are ready for college or the wife wants a McMansion. The bottom line — our line, let's not forget (his eyebrows arched in a perfect pyramid) — is the ultimate test of all reasoning. And if everything else fails, you gentlemen can always drop the s-bomb."

"S-bomb?" the banker asks, edging forward in his seat.

"Sayonara. So long, goodbye, we're off to see the world. What would happen if all four of you suddenly announced you were moving your corporations to—I don't know—India, Brazil, someplace where the taxes are lower, workers cheaper and environmental requirements more welcoming?"

"Panic in the streets," George answers, admiringly.

"Exactly! Gentleman," he says, "it's ours. Our own U.C.A.—the United Corporations of America. We've captured it. For all practical purposes, you own it. Let us drink to our success!" And they all do, in one long draft. Behind them, a bell chimes. Dinner is served.

Everglades Island exists, and Palm Beach on the East Coast of Florida is hardly made up, but the preceding is obviously fiction. Is the scenario far-fetched, though? Let's look at the evidence.

Control of the Institutions of Government

Start with the Executive Branch. Who was Treasury secretary during the closing year of the Clinton administration when the Glass-Steagall Act was taken off the books, allowing banks and investment houses to intermingle assets and treat deposits like casino chips? As we've seen, the answer to that is Robert Rubin, formerly co-chairman of Goldman Sachs, later rewarded by Sandy Weill, who benefited directly from the end of Glass-Steagall, with a $125 million employment-and-directorship package.[96]

Fine. Then who was Treasury secretary as those newly mingled funds were being sliced and diced into every sort of derivative and exchange-traded fund, not to mention bundled packages of sub-prime loans, all of which led inexorably to a financial bubble and the near collapse of the U.S. economy? Well, from 2003 to 2006, that honor belonged to John Snow, former chairman of the Business Roundtable and CEO of CSX, but by the time the Glass-Steagall debris really started hitting the fan, the top Treasury slot was held down by Henry Paulson, former chairman of Goldman Sachs.

Two final questions: Who was the largest institutional contributor to Barack Obama's 2008 presidential campaign? That depends on how you do the math, but if you aggregate all the contributions of its partners, Goldman Sachs would surely win that award, hands down.

And who then became Treasury secretary and helped oversee the disbursement of federal TARP monies to rescue select financial houses brought to their knees by the bubble they helped create? Timothy Geithner, whose previous position as president of the Federal Reserve Bank of New York had made him an intimate of, among others, Bob Rubin and Hank Paulson.

One could read venality into the catechism above, but that's not the issue. Hank Paulson is certainly an honorable person, but inevitably, he viewed the world through the lens of his Goldman experience, and when George W. Bush delegated to him—"abdicated" somehow seems a better word—total responsibility for solving the 2008 financial crisis, Paulson responded by crafting measures that consciously or not were sure to serve the best interests of the one part of the financial economy he understood best: Goldman Sachs.

Nor is the issue particularly political. By most accounts, John McCain was prepared to turn the Treasury department over to Geithner's care had he defeated Obama in 2008. Nor is the issue really that investment bankers generally have controlled the keys to the kingdom in the Obama White House since day one: original Chief of Staff Rahm Emanuel, investment banker at now-extinct Wasserstein Perella & Co.; his successor William Daley, head of Midwest operation for JP Morgan; Daley's successor Jack Lew, hedge fund overseer for Citigroup beginning in 2006 and later chief operating officer of Citi Alternative Investments, where he turned a fortune for the company by investing heavily in John Paulson, who himself made a fortune during the financial crisis by shorting those troubled, often toxic mortgage securities.

Plenty above is troubling, to be sure, but the real issue is the lack of public discomfort with such lines of succession. The real issue is how easily federal oversight of these dangerously exploding financial markets got turned over to the very people whose investment banks played a key role in exploding them as well as to those paid to keep a weather eye on both the markets and their exploiters. Therein lies the essence of capture: it becomes so commonplace, we stop seeing it.

Congress, the second of the sacred triangle of federal governance, is less subtle. The svelte banker above who proposes a toast to Christopher Dodd and Barney Frank is cut of whole cloth, but the fortune spent to defang Dodd-Frank is as real as sin. The Center for Responsive Politics calculates that there were ten lobbyists for each member of the congressional committee charged with writing this new legislation. In the third quarter of 2010 alone—*after* Dodd-Frank had been signed into law—723 clients hired 2,879 lobbyists, virtually all of them focused on excising from the bill's 2,300 pages provisions unacceptable to the business community. And in the end, they succeeded spectacularly.[97]

The independent Consumer Financial Protection Bureau that Elizabeth Warren was originally set to run? It got shrunk down to an agency within the rarely disruptive Federal Reserve (thereby freeing up Warren to run successfully for the U.S. Senate from Massachusetts—an undoubtedly unintended consequence). The so-called "Volcker Rule" meant to keep financial institutions from gambling with their clients' money? It has survived to date, but with exemptions for trusts, insurers, mutual funds, and up to 3 percent of "Tier 1" capital—"a number that for big banks stretches to the billions," as Matt Taibbi pointed out in *Rolling Stone*.[98] And so it went on down the line. What remains is basically the illusion of financial reform, far more acceptable to the financial industry than reform itself.

No American entity other than corporations has the financial resources to wage these sorts of battles, and in the absence of disclosure requirements or any need for approval by shareholders, no one other than the CEOs who run these corporations determines where such money will go. But the compromising of Congress goes far beyond specifically influencing legislation.

A 2010 *New York Times* investigation of federal tax records and House and Senate reports uncovered at least two dozen charities begun by lawmakers and/or their family members and regularly supported by corporate donations. An example: During a six-week period in the fall of 2009, cigarette-maker Altria sent at least $45,000 to four charitable programs, including one founded by then Republican House leader John Boehner and another by then Democratic whip James Clyburn. The company at the time was seeking legislation to curb the Internet sale of cigarettes.[99]

House rules might be expected to avoid such obvious overlaps of interest, if only to avoid the appearance of impropriety, but provisions adopted in 2007 specifically excluded corporate donations to Member's charities. A 2008 measure—the grandly named Honest Leadership and Open Government Act—required lobbyists and lobbying firms to make public their donations to such charities, but transparency did little to stop the flood. The Sunlight Foundation found that, in the two years 2009-2010, special-interest lobbyists contributed $50.2 million to lawmakers' charities and nonprofits, including $6.62 million honoring the Congressional Black Caucus.[100]

Again, this is what capture is all about, less the venality involved—congressmen and senators have had their hands out since Congress began—but the fact that objections are rarely raised to such overt compromises of the legislative process.

As for the judicial branch of government, I have written extensively elsewhere on this subject.[101] Suffice it here to note a 6,466-word analysis drafted by a Richmond, Virginia, lawyer and sent in August 1971 to the chairman of the Education Committee of the U.S. Chamber of Commerce. Under the title "Confidential Memorandum: Attack of American Free Enterprise System," the lawyer laments the "impotency" of the business community in shaping national debate; notes the irony that the attacks on business tend to emanate from campuses "supported by (a) tax funds generated largely from American business, and (b) contributions from capital funds controlled or generated by American business," and from the media, most of which "are owned and theoretically controlled by corporations"; and finally lays out a path forward:

"Business must learn the lesson . . . that political power is
necessary; that such power must be assiduously cultivated; and that
when necessary, it must be used aggressively and with determination—
without embarrassment and without the reluctance which has been so
characteristic of American business."[102]

The lawyer who wrote those words was Lewis Powell, very soon
to be Justice Lewis Powell, and from his memo flows like a mighty
river the bizarre legal reasoning that eventually gave us the majority
opinion in *Citizens United*.

State governments are far more compromised on the whole,
and none more so than Delaware, the tiny slip of a mid-Atlantic
state where nearly half of all publicly traded U.S. companies are
incorporated—and nearly two-thirds of Fortune 500 firms—and where
roughly nine in ten public offerings originate.[103] So accommodating
has Delaware made itself to corporations, that nearly 900,000 business
entities are active there, though "active" in this instance means little
more than a file folder and a mailbox for virtually all of those entities.
A single building at 1209 N. Orange Street in Wilmington houses
somewhere on the order 217,000 companies, including the legal
corporate homes of Coca-Cola, Kentucky Fried Chicken, Google,
Intel, Ford, GM, etc.[104]

Why is the state so popular with corporations? Nicholas Shaxson
answers that question in *Treasure Islands*:

> *Delaware's approach is summed up in its chancery court's
> so-called business judgment rule—under which courts should
> not second-guess corporate managers, provided they did
> not blatantly violate some major rule of conduct and their
> decisions are approved by a "neutral" decision-making body.
> Whatever one thinks of this approach, Delaware has taken it
> to extreme lengths, granting corporate bosses extraordinary
> freedoms from bothersome stockholders, judicial review and
> even public opinion.*[105]

As evidence, Shaxson cites the Delaware chancery court's
dismissal of a suit brought by Walt Disney shareholders seeking to

block the $130 million severance package granted to Michael Ovitz after his dispiriting performance as Disney's CEO. Shareholders, the court ruled, had no right to interfere in board compensation policies—which is to say essentially that in the nation's first state, shareholders have no rights at all.

Far from being the exception, though, Delaware is the rule toward which the nation as a whole is tending. This, too, is what capture is about: Capture exists when the government *becomes* the expression of the business interest, not when it is subjected to business interest—when business interest *subsumes* the government and business purpose becomes the government purpose.

Control of the Instruments of Government

If corporations were to control only the institutions of government, the playing field would be tilted in their direction, but dominion would not be assured. Regulators from football referees to finger-in-the-dike government bureaucrats have a long history of standing bravely in the breech against long odds, raucous fans, and determined, often-moneyed opposition. It's when the *instruments* of government get compromised, or throttled, that the ground truly begins to tremble.

That's where we are now.

Part of the explanation lies in good old-fashioned strong-arming. Here, the most notable (and notorious) case might be that of Gary Aguirre, an SEC investigator who was fired in 2005 for seeking testimony in an insider-trading case from John Mack, soon to become chairman of Morgan Stanley. Aguirre's suspicion—that Mack's former employer, Pequot Capital Management, had profited on information about Heller Financial illegally supplied by Mack—lay dormant for nearly half a decade until being revived by a separate insider-trading action against Pequot, this one involving Microsoft. In 2010, Pequot settled with the SEC for $28 million on that charge and a month later, with little comment, awarded Aguirre $755,000 for wrongful termination.[106]

Part is also explained by what such strong-arm exercises tend to lead to: deliberate forgetfulness and, in the extreme, induced comas. Consider the case of AIG and Joe Cassano. As chief of AIG's financial products subsidiary, Cassano repeatedly claimed in 2007 that his portfolio of high-flying mortgage derivatives would suffer "no dollar of loss"—ridiculous on the face of it and, as things turned out, spectacularly wrong. "God couldn't manage a $60 billion real estate portfolio without a single dollar of loss," Lynn Turner, the SEC's former chief accountant, told *Rolling Stone*. "If the SEC can't make a disclosure case against AIG, then they might as well close up shop." Yet that is exactly what happened. The SEC couldn't (or wouldn't), and they didn't. (And Cassano, for his part, continued to earn $1 million a month as an outside consultant to AIG, even after he was forced out of the company and it was, essentially, owned by the federal government.)[107]

A third element of the story is what explains so much else about the U.C.A.—voluminous, brutal cash. Between 1999 and 2008, the financial sector spent an eye-popping $2.7 billion in lobbying efforts designed to create a close working relationship between bankers and their regulators: "education" programs, retreats, conferences.[108] That again might seem to cross some inviolable line. Imagine, say, the Mafia spending a quarter billion dollars a year to host seminars devoted to organized crime. But criminal justice as it pertains to the Goldmans and Morgan Stanleys of the world is not adversarial combat. Instead, it's a cocktail party between friends and colleagues who from month to month and year to year are constantly switching sides and trading hats.

And little wonder the door does revolve so frequently. An attorney in the SEC's enforcement division might earn $160,000 annually, a pittance in a city like Washington where private-school tuition for two children can run upwards of $70,000 a year. By contrast, a private sector attorney with a thorough knowledge of the SEC and excellent entrée to its enforcement division can charge upwards of $800 an hour for his or her time. Such a lawyer billing 2,000 hours a year—a commonplace figure—would gross in a single year what an SEC lawyer would need a decade to earn. Government lawyers are human. They notice these discrepancies, and they are understandably wary of getting on the wrong side of an industry or its legal representatives for whom they might someday want to work.

In many instances, the regulatory revolving door is built right into the government agency. Employees from pharmaceutical research and lobbying firms, for example, are allowed to rotate through the Food and Drug Administration and then return to their private sector jobs. A 2005 investigation by the Center for Science in the Public Interest found that 10 of the 32 FDA panel members who originally approved the arthritis drug Vioxx, later linked to thousands of deaths, were paid consultants for Merck, which manufactured the drug, and other mainstays of Big Pharma.[109] Not only did the FDA let the foxes in the henhouse; it set aside part of the henhouse for the foxes' comfort—a practice so fundamentally insane that it can be explained only by capture.

Control of the Assumptions Under Which Government Operates

Why do doubts still persist among the American public about the validity of global warming theories and the danger posed by greenhouse gas emissions? Why is the United States the only nation to sign the 1997 Kyoto Protocol but never ratify it, and one of only four UN member states not to do so? (The others: Afghanistan, Andorra, and South Sudan. Canada ratified the protocol but then withdrew from the agreement in December 2011.)[110] The dismal state of basic science education across the nation is certainly a factor but give credit also to one of the least disinterested parties in the world: ExxonMobil, the principal source of funding for virtually all institutions who have published material casting doubt on the science of global warming.

Consider one small instance of Exxon's assault on science: the Arctic Climate Impact Assessment, a landmark international study released in 2004 that combined the work of some 300 scientists, was four years in the making, and called definitively for curbs on greenhouse gasses of the sort emitted by internal-combustion engines powered by, say, ExxonMobil gasoline and lubricated by, say, ExxonMobil motor oil.

John McCain was so concerned by the report's findings that he called for a Senate hearing, more than enough to swing Exxon's mouthpieces into action. Steven Milloy, then an adjunct scholar at the libertarian Cato Institute (which received $90,000 from Exxon between 1998 and 2005) and publisher of the website JunkScience.com, took to the pages of Fox News.com with a debunking opinion piece titled "Polar Bear Scare on Thin Ice." Two days later the right-wing mouthpiece *Washington Times* published the same column. Neither outlet bothered to note that Milloy had founded two organizations that also benefited from ExxonMobil's generosity: the Advancement of Sound Science Center, registered to Milloy's home address in Potomac, Maryland, which received $40,000 in 2002-2003, and Free Enterprise Action Institute, also registered to Milloy's residence, which Exxon supported to the tune of $50,000.[111]

Soon, the conservative George C. Marshall Institute ($630,000 in donations from ExxonMobil between 1998 and 2005) had joined the fray with a press release attacking the Arctic report for "unvalidated" climate models and "scenarios" that bear little resemblance to reality and how the future is likely to evolve. And thus the story continues to this day. In 2010, the U.S. Chamber of Commerce, generously funded by ExxonMobil and many other energy companies, tried mightily to get the EPA to reverse its findings that greenhouse gas emission endangered human health. When that failed, the Chamber sued the agency.[112]

This, too, goes to the very essence of capture: Repeat a bad idea often enough, hire enough mouthpieces to tout it, throw enough conferences to promote the practice whatever it might be, sue when necessary, and you don't have to legislate a thing. Instead, you create an intellectual climate, a buzz, a gestalt in which countervailing concepts are at least stalled if not drowned out entirely.

Thus it was in the 1990s, for example, that accountants accepted the practice of leaving stock options off financial reports, in clear violation of what would be the Hippocratic Oath of the accounting industry if it had one. Thus, too, the shift in much contemporary corporate law scholarship from traditional discourse about protection of investors, to discourse about protection of the corporation from

70

investors. Thus, as the 2011 Oscar-winning documentary *Inside Job* so powerfully points out, prominent economists willingly accepted huge consulting fees in exchange for issuing reports supporting what they had to know was reckless deregulation. And thus we continue today with our bland acceptance of phrases like "creative destruction," the financial industry's favorite oxymoron.

What happens in creative destruction? True, a Staples is occasionally born of the ashes, but far more often, a swarm of MBAs descend on a going industrial concern, saddle it with debt to cover the purchase, pillage the resources, then (a) declare bankruptcy, (b) break the business up and sell the parts, and/or (c) ship the whole enterprise to China or Vietnam or somewhere else where the workers who built the business can and will never go.

We've all seen this movie: The role of the MBAs is played by space aliens; the going industrial concern is a small town, and soon all the townspeople are hollowed-out zombies. But at least in the movies, the aliens get their come-uppance at the end. In real life, the creative destroyers count their wealth in the hundreds of millions of dollars, store it in offshore tax havens, and get to run for president based in large part on their very success at destruction.

Or consider a far more sinister concept that has become embedded in the American conscience: that every decision has to be a servant to the bottom line. This is what happens when economics becomes utterly ascendant. We as Americans used to ask ourselves: Is this the right thing to do or the wrong thing? Now the fundamental question boils down to this: Is it cost effective? And so corporations abrogate long-standing pension agreements because how else can they meet or enhance the bottom line, or not sink any further below it? (Reducing the CEOs' take-home by $10 or $20 million might also help, but that's off the table.) And thus governments state, local, and federal—swept up in the same assumptions—slash spending on education because how else are they to meet or enhance their bottom line, or not sink any further below it? All of which might make sense if people were, in fact, numbers and sacrifice were shared, but they're not, and as everyone knows, it's not either.

Control of the Balance of Power Between Corporations and the Nation-State

So long as there is a balance of power between national and corporate goals, there can be a balance of interests. Yes, CEOs can divert fortunes in shareholder assets in an attempt to elect this president or that. If they are in the insurance industry or HMOs, they can hire armies of lobbyists to assure that the phrase "single payer" is never heard during the debate over health care coverage. Whatever their industry, they can employ SWAT teams of lawyers to create the actual language of laws and regulations governing corporate life and actions, with no assumed obligation to reveal the source of that language. Through grants and other donations and via assiduous courting in other forms, they can encourage academics and op-ed columnists to corrupt the very language by which and through which our civic and economic lives are discussed.

But these things historically have tended to even out over the long run. Corporations go on a spree, CEOs grab for the gold ring, and then the tide turns and populist pressures wash back toward the shore. An Occupy movement springs up. The widening income gap becomes intolerable. This is what balance is all about, and it worked so long as government retained countervailing power to the economic strength of corporations—in the form of taxation, for example, or regulation, or at an extreme the power to seize or even nationalize meaningful assets. One looks in vain for that power today, especially in dealing with the largest multinationals.

An Exxon or a GE earns roughly two-thirds of all revenues outside the United States and retains its offshore profits off-shore as well. Where's the taxing power for the domicile nation in that equation? Halliburton made headlines back in 2007 by shifting its corporate headquarters from Houston to Dubai.[113] Less noted was the fact that roughly 75 percent of the 143 subsidiaries that then made up the Halliburton empire were already registered and operating overseas, in 30 different low-tax (and no-tax) nations.[114] In the United Kingdom, Martin Sorrell has turned all this into a game of sorts, hop-scotching his WPP Group—the British Isles' largest advertising firm—back and forth between London and Dublin, depending on the tax policies and governing parties of the moment. [115]

Catch Sorrell and WPP if you can, but what to catch is almost as great a problem as when, where, and how to catch it. In this new financialized world, there are almost no assets a domicile nation can seize by way of asserting its authority over the owning corporation. Nor is there even a workable bright line any longer between foreign and domestic. Foreign corporations are free to funnel money into the American political process through, say, the U.S. Chamber of Commerce. There's no accounting required; no revelation demanded. Meanwhile, corporations that partake of the nature of foreign entities—that is, they earn the vast majority of their revenues abroad, park most of their profits in offshore tax havens, and are effectively headquartered outside the United States—are entitled by the Supreme Court and the law of the land to openly spend as much as they want to influence U.S. elections in their own favor so long as they are officially domiciled in some convenient mail drop like Delaware.

This is a playing field unlevel in the extreme. For all practical purposes, corporate interests have delineated a boundary within which elected officials can attempt to pursue the public good and beyond which they venture at enormous peril, including the ultimate peril that the corporate interests will skip town—and the country.

Corporations and financial interests, to be sure, have been seeking global advantage for a century and more. Panama began registering foreign ships in 1919, initially mostly to help Standard Oil avoid U.S. regulations and taxes. Wall Street came knocking on Panama's door eight years later, proposing less stringent laws of incorporation than those obtained in the U.S.—as much a boon to the Mob as it was to more legitimate businesses. When former Secretary of State Edward Stettinius, Jr. was drafting a new maritime charter for Liberia in 1948, Standard Oil executives were once more on hand to amend and approve Stettinius's work.[116]

What's different today is not so much the intent as the scale. The off-shoring of yore was mostly about shipping, providing havens for gamblers and for the billions amassed by dictators who didn't dare store their money anywhere close to home. Standard Oil was glad to ship under the Liberian flag, but it wasn't going to beat a corporate retreat to Monrovia. Today, it is far less hard to imagine Standard Oil's successor corporation, ExxonMobil, doing something of the sort. Not to Monrovia, of course—one still needs creature comforts—but perhaps to Rio de Janeiro, if the Brazilians were to wave all tax authority; or to Mumbai if environmental restraints would no longer impede operations.

Plug in the nation you want—of current and future domicile—and the fleeing corporation and the story still comes out pretty much the same. The imbalance between the size and scope of corporate impact and the effective authority of any government to contain it includes, and is in many ways even premised upon, holding nations hostage to threats of relocation and related job and tax loss unless they turn themselves into tax havens, and in the process virtually assuring on a global scale the tax loss each nation individually is seeking to avoid. According to research by the British-based Enough Food for Everyone IF Campaign, closing the "corporation tax gap" in developing countries would "raise enough public revenues to save the lives of 230 children every six minutes, one child every six seconds."[117] The race to the bottom among nations has ultimately only one winner: the corporations that own the starting gun and set the finish line.

This is where we have arrived. Over the past several decades, national governments have seen the most basic pillars of their power erode. Globalization has undermined efforts to manage their borders. The ability to control their own currency has been lost for all but a handful of major powers. Fewer than two dozen nations have the ability to project sustainable force beyond their borders.

Meanwhile, corporations play nation-states against one another as they venue-shop for more attractive tax or regulatory regimes. This arbitrage undermines nations' ability to enforce their own laws. Indeed, the rise of big stateless corporations, which now rival many countries in terms of economic and political clout, poses special new challenges to governments.

Time magazine caught the spirit of this new age, and the challenges, with a February 2012 opinion piece by "Curious

74

Capitalist" columnist Rana Foroohra titled "Companies Are the New Countries." Patriotism is on life support, the bottom line rules, and even the good news that some American corporations are bringing jobs home is ultimately bad, according to the article. A survey of 10,000 Harvard Business School alumni found that most of those responsible for repatriating jobs are doing so for rational, not national reasons. (Indeed, the article might have been titled "Profitism Is the New Patriotism.") If there was a "metatheme" to the 2012 World Economic Forum at Davos, Foroohra writes, it was "that the world's largest companies are moving beyond governments and countries that they perceive to be inept and anemic."[118]

Ownership, in short, is global. Corporate functioning is global. Yet no political instrumentality, not even the United States, is global. That leaves us tiptoeing through a world in which the power of multinational corporations is utterly asymmetrical with the power of the countries in which they are domiciled. And that inevitably leaves Americans and others at the whim of the informing energy of the corporations that increasingly hold them hostage.

Question: What is the informing energy of this new U.C.A.?

****

5.
Greed Is, Like, Awesome!

The point is, ladies and gentleman, that greed, for lack of a better word, is good. Greed is right, greed works. Greed clarifies, cuts through, and captures the essence of the evolutionary spirit. Greed, in all of its forms; greed for life, for money, for love, knowledge, has marked the upward surge of mankind. And greed, you mark my words, will not only save Teldar Paper, but that other malfunctioning corporation called the USA.

— Gordon Gekko

Gordon Gekko's speech, masterfully delivered by Michael Douglas in Oliver Stone's 1987 film *Wall Street*, remains memorable to this day. In only 74 words, just at the end of a riveting 3-minute, 18-second oration, Gekko seemed to capture the spirit of an entire era. Corporate raiders were liberators, not destroyers. They rescued decaying enterprises from stagnant management, restored them to vitality, and returned them to their owners, the shareholders, as the profit-churning machines they should have been all along. For that, of course, the raiders—the Gekkos, the Carl Icahns and others in real life—were more than handsomely rewarded, but without the promise of reward they would not have been motivated to act in the first place. Greed was their informing energy. It got the raiders up in the morning; it put them to bed at night. Greed is what they lived for, what they dreamed of, but the thing is, it *worked*.

Twenty-five years later, an anonymous Apple executive unwittingly redefined greed for our own era when he told the *New York Times*: "We sell iPhones in over a hundred countries. We don't have an obligation to solve America's problems. Our only obligation is making the best product possible."[119]

This is what greed looks like in the global epoch of corporatism: plunder the treasury, to be sure, but then deny all sense of responsibility to your country of domicile, outsource all obligations, and like maggots, set to work destroying the host from inside by exporting its jobs and depleting its revenue sources.

Apple might be the most admired company on the planet right now—one of the world's most efficient money-making machines. In 2011, the company earned $400,000 per employee—better than Goldman Sachs, better than ExxonMobil, better than Google. And it's certainly a global company: Virtually all the 159 million *things* Apple sold in 2011 were made somewhere other than in America. Roughly a third of its employees—20,000 of 63,000 total—are also overseas, a percentage that soars dramatically if you include the 700,000 additional people involved in turning out Apple products for an almost infinite network of contractors.[120]

But does that make Apple, in effect, an independent nation within the larger political entity of the United States? Clearly it does so in the mind of the anonymous company executive interviewed by the *New York Times*. But not when we step back and look at the larger picture. Clyde Prestowitz, founder and head of the Economic Strategy Institute, did just that in a January 23, 2012, posting on the *Foreign Policy* website:

In the 1981-86 period I was one of the U.S. government's top trade negotiators, especially with Japan. At that time, Apple was trying to crack the Japanese market for personal computers and getting nowhere. Steve Jobs and other Apple executives had the funny notion that the U.S. government had an obligation to help them and asked me and other negotiators at the Commerce Department and the Office of the U.S. Trade Representative to help them get on the shelf in Japan. We did all we could and in doing so came to learn that virtually everything Apple had for sale, from the memory chips to the cute pointer mouse, had had its origins in some program wholly or partially supported by U.S. government money.

*Nor have things changed that much in the intervening time.
Apple's products still have a large U.S. government R&D
content and I'll bet that the guy who says Apple has no
obligation to help Uncle Sam does strongly believe that
Uncle Sam has an obligation to stop foreign pirating of
Apple's intellectual property and to maintain the deployments
of the U.S. Seventh Fleet and of the 100,000 U.S. troops in
the Asia-Pacific region that make it safe for Apple to use
supply chains that stretch through a number of countries such
as China and Japan between which there are long standing
and bitter animosities.* [121]

Apple, or at least its let-them-eat-cake executive quoted in the
Times, seems to have found itself on third base and assumed not only
that it hit a triple but that it manufactured the bat and the ball, laid out
the base paths, and built the stadium. The Business Roundtable, of
which Apple is not a member, takes that argument a step further. The
high-flying CEOs who comprise BRT share Apple's assumptions but
also take it as a given that having landed on third base, they now have
the right to tell everyone else how to play the game.

Consider first this bland passage from the preface to BRT's 2010
"Roadmap for Growth":

*As CEOs of our nation's largest companies, Business
Roundtable members know that it is essential to our future
domestic success that American businesses are competitive
at home and abroad. We stand ready to work with lawmakers
to help achieve a common understanding of the unforeseen
consequences that poorly considered regulation and
legislation can have on the competitiveness of American
businesses, and on the country's ability to remain a global
economic leader and create new jobs. We are prepared
to work with elected officials to help define clear policies
that will make the future more certain and businesses more
optimistic.* [122]

Then look at the specific ways in which BRT would "grow"
America to the future:

79

The first way, a given, is to lower the corporate tax rate, implement comprehensive reform of the entire corporate tax system, and reinstate and extend business tax incentives that expired during the financial crisis of 2008 and its aftermath.

Thus, in one form or another, those corporations domiciled in the U.S. that have not yet figured out how to offshore all their profits will be paying fewer taxes on the profits that remain should the BRT's plan for growth be enacted. Reasonably, then, they might expect fewer services and less support from their domicile's government. These are people who live on a steady diet of *quid pro quo*. But that's not the way this game works.

International market access? The BRT wants—indeed it all but demands—that the U.S. "aggressively pursue trade and investment agreements" and "*aggressively* enforce U.S. rights under international agreements." (Emphasis added, in both cases, but clearly understood.) Also on the BRT agenda: strengthening intellectual property protection and increasing energy security while (and one can almost hear the authors laughing at this point) "addressing environmental concerns." And so it continues.

American education, the report in essence says, is abysmal. Statistics agree, but funding the proposed solutions, better math and science education, better K-12 education, etc., goes unmentioned in the report.

Energy? Expand the grid (also unfunded), maintain coal as a viable option, and let the foxes into the henhouse once again so corporations can write environmental regulations collaboratively with government agencies.

Financial regulations and SEC rulemaking? More henhouses, more foxes. Dump the proxy access the SEC awarded significant shareholders. (This, as we've seen, has since been accomplished.) "Avoid overregulation of derivatives." "Make certain that the final rules add value, enhance confidence in the economy and foster companies' ability to grow and create jobs"—i.e., that there are still more "final" rules long after the legislation has been passed, à la Dodd

Frank, that create the illusion of regulation as opposed to its reality.[123]

Finally, this is what the BRT "Roadmap" comes down to: Tax us less, give us more, return us to the regulatory climate that brought on the Great Recession and the environmental nightmare that was the Gulf of Mexico for half a year and lingers still, and *get the hell out of the way*. All of which might be grimly laughable and utterly predictable if it weren't also so emblematic of the citizenship these new corporate persons are demanding for themselves—not one of shared burden, not one of country first, but a citizenship driven entirely by the bottom line, the culmination of a trend in corporate *realpolitik* that has been decades in the making.

Externalizing for Fun and Profit

Imagine neighbors who regularly toss their garbage bags over the fence for you to dispose of; neighbors whose teenage children throw drunken orgies whenever the parents leave town—the sound system at full blast, beer cans strewn over your lawn in the morning along with a passed-out underage partier or two; neighbors who pirate your wireless signal, who connect their hoses to your outdoor faucets to water their *own* lawn and shrubs, who make sure *their* dogs do their business on *your* little patch of green verge by the street and never clean up after them; neighbors who pluck your daffodils in spring for their kitchen table, your ripe tomatoes in summer for their salads, and your precious dahlias in September just because they can, without asking and never so much as a thank you.

Then imagine that these neighbors are well connected. His brother-in-law is the local police chief. Her sister runs the town council. There's an uncle who publishes the local newspaper. You can complain—this is America—but no one will hear.

Imagine all that, and you basically have the externalized world that America's largest corporations occupy today.

Once, corporations saw it both as their obligation and in their economic self-interest to create and sustain a stabilizing middle class.

81

Henry Ford's great success was built in part on his decision to pay his workers a high enough wage so that they could afford the products they were producing. No more. The shrinking middle class, the widening gap between the rich and the poor—these are some of those American "problems" that American-born-and-bred corporations like Apple really have no time for.

Once, it was a given that America's largest corporations would look after their employees in their golden years. Unions demanded as much, of course, but an earlier generation of CEOs did more than cave in. Faithful service deserved faithful care and stewardship. Besides, this is what it meant to be in the American melting pot together—one for all, all for one, a chain of associations only as strong as its weakest link. No more here either. The BRT's "Roadmap" waxes grandly on reforming Social Security and empowering workers with self-directed investments, but behind it all lies a very loud "Whew! Thank God, we're out of that business." And are they ever!

Today, the federal Pension Benefit Guaranty Corporation, not private industry, is on the hook for nearly $7 billion annually in defined benefit pensions that have been shed by American companies, largely through bankruptcy proceedings that are too often little more than shell games. Case in point: Friendly's, the family-oriented restaurants/ice-cream parlors. In 2008, Friendly's was taken private by equity firm Sun Capital. Three years later, Friendly's filed for protection under Chapter 11 of the federal bankruptcy laws. There, its pension obligations to its roughly 6,000 employees were shifted to the PBGC, and then Friendly's, now unencumbered, was sold to—ta-da!—an affiliate of Sun Capital.[124] In the rackets, this is known as money laundering. In the C-Suites of the Palace of Private Equity, you would have to be a chump *not* to play the system for all it's worth.

Health and environmental costs have a deeper and more complicated history, but one no less unsavory. Corporations have been externalizing this red ink since the advent of the Industrial Revolution and double-entry bookkeeping. Cigarette manufacturers, to cite one obvious example, extract the profit potential inherent in tobacco products, while outsourcing to tobacco users and the public at large the demonstrable health and productivity results of smoking: lung cancer, emphysema, a host of issues associated with secondary smoke inhalation, lost work days, etc.

Coal externalizes even more effectively. Mining companies extract the value inherent in coal, while shifting the consequences of actually extracting it to the miners themselves—black lung, cave-ins, and the like—and then on to government when the coal miners can no longer pay for their own care. Once the coal is above ground, utilities burn it to reap the profits inherent in its energy potential, while outsourcing the known environmental degradation and greenhouse gas consequences of combusting fossil fuels to the public, and increasingly the planet at large.

This is the essence of externalization. Financial burdens—whether for pensions, education, retraining, health, the demolition of abandoned structures, the restoration (or preservation) of the environment—are either shifted to government or made to be borne by the workers themselves or the general public. Whoever ultimately bears the burden—so long as it is not the entity that generates it—externalizing these costs is the functional equivalent of an increase of profits. Share prices rise, market-cap value ascends. Corporate managers are rewarded accordingly, and the only ones who suffer are all the rest of us: governments federal, state, and local and workers themselves, all of whom increasingly cannot meet the costs that corporations are shifting to them.

As economist Neva Goodwin has pointed out, "Power is largely what externalities are about. What's the point of having power if you can't use it to externalize your costs—to make them fall on someone else?"[125]

A Corporate Tax on America

Once, in what seems almost a fairytale time, externalization was recognized for the corporate tax on the public that it is, and government set about to achieve redress. To help remedy disasters such as Love Canal that could no longer be ignored, Congress in 1980 passed the Comprehensive Environmental Response Compensation and Liability Act—better known as Superfund. The Hazard Ranking System followed in 1981 and, the next year, a National Priorities List. A Superfund trust was created to tackle the sites, with the funds coming from taxes on petroleum and related chemical products, since these were far and away the largest sources of the pollution the Act was meant to correct. This, of course, was not the same as actually getting the money from the polluters—they were able to externalize the obligation to their customers, but even that was too much. Lobbyists got cracking, campaign financing was fine-tuned, the corporate dream-machine kicked into full gear, and things just petered away.

The tax disappeared in 1995. EPA still attempts to find the specific companies responsible for individual sites, but even when it does find them, the companies don't have to report back to the agency how much they have spent on the effort. (Imagine, for example, a paroled sex offender forced to wear a monitoring device that neither records location nor reports it anywhere.)

When responsible parties cannot be found, the Superfund picks up the tab, but the Superfund is dwindling. Over the decade ending in 2010, it allocated $243 million annually in clean-up funding; EPA estimates that anywhere from $335 million to $681 million annually will be needed for future cleanup.[126] Even at the top figure, that sum equals a little more than 2 percent of the annual sales of a single chemical company, Dow, and less than .2 percent of the annual sales of ExxonMobil, but for the federal government, for taxpayers, for states and localities, seeing the Superfund's work through to completion looks to be a cost too far.

Meanwhile, as of February 2011 one in four Americans was still living within three miles of a contaminated Superfund site that poses serious risks to human health and the environment, according to the Environmental Protection Agency.

There is, after all, a moral dimension to externalization, a moral dimension to the bottom-line-at-all-costs, feed-the-beasts-of-management-first mentality that is greed in our own times. The Superfund is one illustration. Plenty of others can be cited.

Take Hostess Brands. When the maker of iconic Twinkies, Ding Dongs, and Devil Dogs shuttered its doors in November 2012, much media attention was paid to the intransigence of one of its unions—the Bakery, Confectionary, Tobacco Workers and Grain Millers International—whose members refused to accept a new contract that would have slashed their salaries while gutting retirement benefits.

Yet, as Helaine Olen noted on the Forbes website, Hostess Brands management had rewarded itself with multiple raises as the bakery slipped into and out of bankruptcy over the last decade. Nor has management itself yet gone out of business. While 18,000 Hostess workers are likely to join the ranks of the unemployed—unless a last-minute mediation effort breaks the logjam—the company's executive team will be selling its famous brands off to the highest bidders. Thus, management outsources the pain of failure to the workers who kept the business going, while taking one last bite out of the enterprise. That, too, goes to the heart of greed in our time—the asymmetric imposition of pain.[127]

Or consider the appalling history of major pharmaceutical firms over the last half decade. As of this writing, five of the leading lights of the business have agreed to settlements of more than a billion dollars each in cases involving everything from illegal marketing practices to selling drugs for uses for which they have not been approved and otherwise endangering the health, even the lives of consumers.

Eli Lilly settled civil and criminal charges to the tune of $1.4 billion in 2009. Pfizer followed the same year with a settlement of $2.3 billion. Then came GlaxoSmithKline ($3 billion), Abbott ($1.5 billion), and most recently Johnson & Johnson (somewhere north of $1 billion.) Amgen narrowly missed the billion dollar club when it got off the hook for a light-as-a-feather $750 million in October 2011.[128]

Do these fines come out of the pocket of the executives who approve the practices that result in the penalties? Of course not. They're an expected part of business, priced broadly into product lines. In effect, Eli Lilly, Pfizer, and the others have externalized the cost of their malfeasance and in some cases outright criminality to their own customer base.

Or consider BP. The 2010 Deepwater Horizon explosion and wellhead rupture was not the company's first debacle in the immediate region. Five years earlier, an explosion at the company's Texas City refinery killed 15 employees and injured, and in some cases badly maimed, another 170 people.

Following the Texas City disaster, I was retained as an expert witness by the plaintiffs in an action brought by injured parties. The extent of the damage was impossible to ignore, and it was clear that this couldn't simply be brushed under the rug and huge monies paid to make it go away. The problems were far too pervasive for that — it really was a question of the *culture* of British Petroleum.

BP had grown very aggressively under Lord John Brown by buying American companies, mostly on the cheap when oil prices were down. Unhappily, the low price of oil and the general culture at BP meant that the principal management mandate was cut expenses. Costs were pared ruthlessly in the area of safety, and there was no question that this was a contributing factor in the fire at the Texas City refinery, where there had been an absence of training, supervision, and capital investment.[129]

Coming out of any corporate disaster, the usual procedure is to hire a prestigious law firm to investigate and then issue an opinion that in effect says, "You've been bad boys, but you're working very hard to fix it and nobody should go to jail." To that end, BP hired one of the best in the business, former Secretary of State Jim Baker, and he wrote such a report. But at the end of the report Baker spoke about a failure of a culture of safety; he specifically recommended that the board of directors appoint one particular director to be in charge of this and that they impose upon themselves a mandate of achieving workplace safety for all employees.[130]

BP appeared to take this seriously. In its 2006 annual report, the company promised, "Our long-term goals are 'no accidents, no harm to people, and no damage to the environment.' We have made it clear that: Everyone who works for BP, anywhere, is responsible for getting HSE right. We have put Health, Safety and Environmental management systems and processes into place to help us live up to these aspirations."[131]

And then, of course, five years later, disaster—human and this time environmental—not only struck a second time, but subsequent investigations have shown that while BP had improved its public-relations effort, it hadn't altered its culture a bit. Personnel were negligent, perhaps criminally so; procedures were not up to the mark. In all, the company has now pleaded guilty to 11 counts of misconduct or negligence. Two senior managers aboard the drilling platform have been charged with manslaughter and a third company official with obstructing a congressional investigation. Once the total tab is in, BP might end up paying out as much as $50 billion across a vast array of fines and penalties. But the point is, it's *just* money—and BP has oodles of it. [132]

Of course, no company can absorb a $50 billion hit without at least blinking, but oil trans-nationals like BP have so much money in reserve—intentionally built into the business plan, held back for moments just like this—that fines and penalties even of this size are more annoying than debilitating. In the end, they take no real responsibility for the long-term damage, and there is no long-term damage to their business.

Meanwhile, there's the grim tally of the people, places, and things made to bear the real burden of conducting an inherently dangerous enterprise with insufficient safety procedures: BP's own workers, eleven of whom died in the Deepwater Horizon explosion; the Upper Gulf fishing industry, which was decimated by the still untallied millions of barrels of oil released into the water; an entire ecosystem that found itself on the brink of ruin; and inevitably the customers of BP products, who have found and will continue to find BP's potential $50 billion in fines and penalties built into every gallon of gas they pump.

This is immoral.

Greed, National Interest, and Corporate Interests

Greed, in fact, can be good. Coupled with innovation and ambition, greed has long been the driving force of capitalist democracy. People act because they want, because they are ambitious. They innovate to explore and conquer new seams in the market. And in doing so, they create enterprises, sometimes great and lasting ones, that employ millions, become the rallying point for communities, the ladder up out of poverty in the ongoing social experiment of America.

In broad terms, Gordon Gekko had it just right. But *Wall Street* hit the theaters a quarter century ago. Today, under the reign of self-enriching manager-kings, greed alone is ascendant. Greed untempered by innovation and ambition is the informing energy of the corpocracy.

Evidence? What we have been looking at throughout this book: the offloading of all externalities; the abrogation of social responsibilities in the form of pensions, health care, stewardship of the environment, and on and on; the off-shoring of production that has created what seems to be a new permanent class of the able unemployed; the off-shoring of corporate headquarters and accounts in pursuit of laxer regulation and favorable taxation; the way so many CEOs treat their corporations as personal ATM machines, with no limit on withdrawals; maybe most dramatically, the simple fact that the greatest "innovation" in American corporate life today can be found not in the manufacturing sector but in the creation of financial instruments that are themselves little more than MBA-certified Ponzi schemes in which the house has every advantage.

National interests and corporate interests were once understood to occupy separate spheres in our communal life. Dwight Eisenhower raised the subject memorably with his comments on the military-industrial-scientific complex. Today, under the three-fold pressures of relentless lobbying, a compliant Court and Congress, and a political system flooded with corporate cash, the two interests are widely seen as one and the same. Corporations view tax payments and compliance with the law as matters to be determined by spread sheet. They refuse to constructively engage in efforts to enhance accounting practices that are clearly in the public interest—the appropriate recognition of externalities, for examples, and incentives for management to pursue policies in aid of the common good. "Good citizenship" is now widely believed to be a *numerical* measurement, not a fulfillment of civic obligation, but the issue is far bigger than that.

In this merger of national and business interests, corporations have seized the power to direct and allocate public resources into (their own) private hands. Look at the mining raid on public lands. Look at how space exploration has been turned over to the private sector. NASA, heaven knows, had problems, but the fruits of its innovations—and they were legendary—were public property, with a modest access fee. Those days, at least for now, are far, far away in a distant galaxy.

Look, too, at the fundamentally insane assumptions behind so much of the Business Roundtable's "Roadmap for Growth": that the EPA and industry should "collaboratively" come up with environmental regulations, that the SEC and industry should jointly decide on what's good and bad for the air we breathe, the water we drink, the financial institutions to which we entrust our savings, and the like.[133] Isn't the BP object lesson enough on that front? Did we learn nothing from the near financial meltdown of 2008? How did self-regulation work when banks in 2011 were in essence allowed to determine on their own what constituted wrongful mortgage foreclosures and what the redress should be? Answer: They spent $1.5 billion on consultants who found little wrong and thus almost no need for redress, and eventually settled with the Federal Reserve and the Office of the Comptroller of the Currency for a package of penalties that comes nowhere near equaling the malfeasance involved, not to mention the human pain caused.[134]

We even use corporations today to expand and protect empire, an absolute abrogation of public duty and responsibility. Want to fight a war? Find the right price point to lure a sufficient number of "volunteer" soldiers to duty, staff the green zone with independent contractors, and go to it. To heck with the public will, with the hard, hard business of deciding collectively if this is a war worth fighting and, equally important, if anyone wants to fund it.

The war metaphor is not by chance. Corporations today more closely resemble unmanned drones than anything an Ike would recognize. Indeed, the drone corporation is emerging as the first truly legitimate "institutional claimant of significant unregulated power since the nation-state established its title in the 16th and 17th centuries."[135] Like its namesake weapon, the multinational corporation has vast power. It externalizes collateral damage. Neither weapon nor corporation is subject to terrestrial restraints. And both are controlled remotely by a small body of persons entirely removed from the consequences of their actions.

Question: How is this working for investors?

****

6.
Drone Corporations

If greed untempered by other considerations of the public good were the measure of a corporation's ability to compete in the new dog-eat-dog global economy, then it would stand to reason that enterprises of the sort I have just been describing—what I've come to think of as "drone corporations"—would best serve investors. After all, this is the argument most often advanced in defense of manager-controlled enterprises operating in a maximally unregulated environment: that the more free CEOs are to concentrate on profit, the more aligned their own interests are with the bottom line, and the more they can externalize all risks to the public at large, the greater the returns will be for *all* stakeholders: employees up and down the line, shareholders, community, country.

But is it so?

To find out, we undertook a study to my knowledge never before attempted: a comparison of "drone" and "non-drone" corporations over a wide range of performance metrics. The study was headed up by Ric Marshall, chief analyst of GMIRatings, a company I helped form in 2010 to address systemic shortfalls in the understanding of risks facing public companies. Full results of the study, including a detailed description of the methodology, are available at http://www.governmentcapture.com/citizens-disunited. We'll get to extensive highlights soon, but first, some background and definitions.

Distributed ownership is the essence of democratic capitalism. In the capital markets of Anglo-America, the widely held corporation is by far the most common form, with founder- or family-controlled companies comprising less than 15 percent of all public corporations. But a majority of public companies in these markets still retain some semblance of focused ownership, some remnant of vested interest and concern. Among larger companies, though, this is no longer the case. It was this group that we particularly sought to probe—corporations so widely owned and so widely traded that, in effect, they have no owners.

Most simply stated, the drone corporation is one in which no single shareholder retains a principal position, defined by the SEC as 10 percent or more. In most cases the largest single position is likely to be less than half that amount, or it may be held by a shareholder that is, itself, also widely held, such as a mutual fund or a passive index fund. In the most radical cases, the largest single position may be less than one percent of the shares outstanding.

The 10 percent test was one of three screens applied to all companies in the S&P 500 as of the end of June 2012. These screens also excluded any company in which:

- One or more founders continue to play a key guidance role as either CEO or chairman, regardless of the size of this individual's holdings.

- Family interests, in most cases linked to the company's founder, are represented by active board members, regardless of the size of the family's current holdings

The intent was to separate out companies with one or more vested owners, or more specifically shareholders, whose holdings were of sufficient size and importance to warrant, perhaps even compel, an active level of monitoring and participation in the affairs of the corporation. The results divided the S&P 500 into two quite different corporate groups: corporate drones where passive ownership is the rule—269 of the 500 companies studied—and companies with one or more active, vested owners, the non-drones, 229 corporations in all. (The status of two of the corporations studied could not be determined.)

While drones are not alone in placing primary focus on the bottom line, inserting themselves into our political and regulatory systems, and practicing externalization, non-drones necessarily get there with the approval, tacit or explicit, of vested owners and family/founder interests. Corporate drones resolve the agency problems inherent in the public form by simply eliminating vested owners from the equation, and by elevating the power and authority of the CEO and board accordingly. Drones are thus the ultimate expression of the corporate form darkly envisioned by Louis Brandeis, enterprises in which "ownership has been separated from control."

Who are the drones? Their ranks include some of the most powerful, influential, and best-known companies in America. Here are the fifty largest, ranked by market cap, as of August 15, 2012:[136]

1. ExxonMobil Corporation
2. International Business Machines Corporation
3. General Electric Company
4. Chevron Corporation
5. AT&T Inc.
6. Procter & Gamble Company (The)
7. Johnson & Johnson
8. Wells Fargo & Company
9. JPMorgan Chase & Co.
10. Pfizer Inc.
11. Coca-Cola Company (The)
12. Philip Morris International Inc.
13. Intel Corporation
14. Merck & Co., Inc.
15. QUALCOMM Incorporated
16. Cisco Systems, Inc.
17. Verizon Communications Inc.
18. Citigroup Inc.
19. PepsiCo, Inc.
20. Bank of America Corporation
21. McDonald's Corporation
22. ConocoPhillips
23. Abbott Laboratories
24. Visa Inc.
25. Schlumberger Limited
26. Walt Disney Company (The)

27. United Parcel Service, Inc.
28. Occidental Petroleum Corporation
29. Kraft Foods Inc.
30. Altria Group, Inc.
31. 3M Company
32. EMC Corporation
33. UnitedHealth Group Incorporated
34. U.S. Bancorp
35. CVS Caremark Corporation
36. Bristol-Myers Squibb Company
37. Amgen Inc.
38. Union Pacific Corporation
39. E.I. du Pont de Nemours and Company
40. Hewlett-Packard Company
41. Colgate-Palmolive Company
42. Accenture plc
43. Monsanto Company
44. Medtronic, Inc.
45. Anadarko Petroleum Corporation
46. Lowe's Companies, Inc.
47. Target Corporation
48. Southern Company (The)
49. Apache Corporation
50. Texas Instruments Incorporated

This list includes America's largest banks; its biggest oil companies; its leading communication, chemical, and pharmaceutical companies, and a wide-ranging assortment of key consumer goods and entertainment providers. These top 50 drone corporations—just 10 percent of the full S&P 500—represent nearly $5.2 trillion in market capitalization, approximately 40 percent of the S&P 500's total aggregate market cap. The CEOs of 35 of the top 50 sit on the Business Roundtable. Of the top 20, all but two, Wells Fargo and Philip Morris, belong to the BRT.[137]

The correlation between drone corporations and the Business Roundtable is neither immaterial nor gratuitous. Drones are both the creations and bastions of the CEOs who set and control the BRT agenda, and paradigms of the corporate model aspired to by these same CEOs and their co-lobbyists, including the U.S. Chamber of Commerce. Thus, one can reasonably inquire—and indeed should inquire—how achieving drone status expresses itself in management, corporate governance, behavior, and performance, especially as compared with non-drones.

We start with management.

Drone CEOs: Up the Ladder, Well Protected, and Royally Paid

• While the average tenure of corporate drone CEOs is more than two years shorter than at non-drones, the drone CEO is far more likely to be a "company man," one who rose up through the ranks of the company by way of more junior positions.

• Despite their shorter average tenure, drone CEOs are almost 50 percent more likely to be named Chairman of the Board as well.

• Drone CEOs took home last year, on average, approximately $1.25 million more than non-drone chief executives. Adjusted on the basis of average total returns, drone CEOs out-earned their non-drone counterparts by nearly 50 percent.[138]

This is, we're told, the age of permanent churn. Multiple employers, even multiple careers are the rule, not the exception. If so, drone CEOs are the exception to the exception. They tend to ascend through the ranks, patiently being groomed until the C-Suite is finally available to them.

Michael Laphen, former CEO and Chairman of Computer Science Corporation, is illustrative. After 30 years with the firm in ever more important positions, Laphen reached the top of the company and the board chair in 2007. Four years later, at age 61, he announced his retirement. His last full year as CEO/chairman, Laphen took home $21 million, despite Computer Sciences' underperforming both its industry peers and the S&P 500 as a whole throughout his entire tenure at the helm. Laphen's fiscal 2012 total summary compensation was over eight times the median total summary compensation paid to each of Computer Sciences' next four highest paid executives. Laphen also received $6.75 million in cash severance payments at his departure and, due to his long service with the company, will enjoy an additional $15 million in accumulated pension benefits.[139]

And so it goes down the line: long service and Midas-like rewards at the end, all too frequently divorced from performance. Of the CEOs of the top six drone corporations as measured by market cap, only one had tenure in excess of ten years: GE's Jeffrey Immelt. Only one was not a company man: Proctor & Gamble's Robert McDonald. And none had total compensation in 2011 of less than $16 million. A different story gets told by the CEOs of the top six non-drone corporations, again as measured by market cap: Apple, Microsoft, Google, Wal-Mart, Oracle, and Berkshire Hathaway. Four of the six had tenure of 12 years or more. None was a company man, although most had played a key role in launching the company, and none had total compensation in excess of $18 million.

One could argue that the above is an apples-and-oranges comparison. The top drones are long-established entities, while the non-drones are relative startups. Further five of the six non-drone CEOs as of 2011, the last date for which total compensation is available, had huge founder stakes in their companies. Annual compensation was hardly an issue for them.

But to a large extent, apples-and-oranges *is* the point here. Several of the top six non-drone CEOs are famously contentious or outspoken: Larry Ellison at Oracle, the eminently quotable Warren Buffett at Berkshire Hathaway. Some are just plain quirky or borderline anti-social. Like Apple's Steve Jobs, Google's Larry Page was frequently late for meetings during his first stint as the company's CEO and even more frequently bored by what he heard. Like Jobs, too, Page was brought back for a second run in the top position.

The drone CEOs by contrast are courtiers. They achieved their present positions mostly by impressing and pleasing their superiors within the company. Having been elevated to the top management position, they also secured the chairmanship so in the future they would mostly have to please themselves. Their emotional stake in the business might well be as great as that of any founder, but their claim on the corporate treasury is largely determined by (a) manipulating short-term results, not building long-term strengths into the enterprise, and (b) structuring severance and/or retirement packages that will assure an undiminished standard of living no matter what the future might hold.

This is a formula for self-referential thinking, not creative action. Drone boards only make matters worse.

Drone Boards: Interlocking Directorates, Powerful Chairmen, Tenuous Commitment

- Drones are more likely to have other, active corporate CEOs on their boards.

- Drones are also more likely to have present and former CEOs on their compensation committees.

- Non-executive director shareholdings at corporate drone boards average less than half the dollar value of their non-drone counterparts.

Boards are at their strongest when they merge expertise, fresh perspectives, and a willingness to speak out with the iron-clad obligation to best serve the interests of the shareholders who elected them. They are far worse when they do little more than reflect the will of a CEO/chairman who hand selects directors either because of ongoing peer-to-peer friendships or assumed entrée to the capital markets in New York and the marble portals of the nation's capital. And they are at their absolute worst when directors sit on one another's boards, and the directorates themselves begin to interlock and serve mutual corporate interests rather than the specific interests of shareholders of the individual entities.

These "worse" and "worst" situations are true to a remarkable degree of the intricate networks of director connections that revolve around all four of the largest U.S. banks: Wells Fargo, J.P. Morgan Chase, Citigroup, and Bank of America, drones every one. Over the past two decades ago, these four banks have been cobbled together out of 37 separate financial-related institutions. But the consolidation is inter-bank as well. JP Morgan Chase owns a 1.8 percent stake in Wells Fargo, a 1.82 percent stake in Citigroup, and a 2.09 percent stake in Bank of America. (BlackRock has a stake in all four banks greater than 2.5 percent.) Today, it's less the individual banks than the sector itself that is "too big to fail" since one bank failure has the potential to affect all four, hence the remnants of all 37, and hence *every one*.[140]

Externally, the boards of the four banks connect, via one or more shared directors, with 58 other companies. Wells Fargo's directors' network alone includes the boards of 21 other public companies of which at least a third are themselves drones. Two of these drone boards—Chevron and Target—share not one but two individual directors. One is the current CEO of Wells Fargo, John Stumpf, who doubles as chairman of the Wells Fargo board. Not including Stumpf, seven of Wells Fargo's fifteen directors are themselves either current or former CEOs, including the chairman of the compensation committee that oversees Stumpf's pay.

The four boards are also closely tied to multiple presidential administrations, regulatory agencies, and advisory commissions. Collectively, they include two former Cabinet members, a former member of the Federal Reserve Board of Governors, an ex-chairwoman of the Board of the Federal Reserve Bank of San Francisco, a one-time chairman of the Federal Deposit Insurance Corporation, several ex-Cabinet undersecretaries, the president of the Rockefeller Foundation, a director of the W.K. Kellogg Foundation, and other luminaries, including Crandall Bowles, chairman of Springs Industries and the wife of former White House Chief of Staff Erskine Bowles, better known today for his key role in the Simpson-Bowles Commission.[141]

Lay these sweeping board connections out in graphic form and the result is a thing of beauty—a banking industry with sinuous connections into virtually every element of the economy and its overseers and regulators. But the question has to be asked: Do these four monster drone banks with their exquisitely credentialed directorates serve their shareholders, their customers, their communities, and/or their nation more effectively than their 37 predecessor organizations did? On this score, the evidence is decidedly negative. All four played a central role in the subprime-mortgage debacle that brought the national economy to its knees. Two—Citigroup and BOA—had to be rescued by American taxpayers. JP Morgan was up to its ears in the Enron and WorldCom debacles of a decade ago. Much more recently, the bank acknowledged mortgage overcharges on the families of military personnel serving in Afghanistan. Wells Fargo, which benefited from federal bailout money in the wake of the financial crisis, has been under almost constant assault by various governmental agencies for false claims, alleged discrimination, etc.[142]

True, the job of a board isn't to wade too far into the weeds of management, but directors are charged with assuring the right CEO is in place and setting the right tone, and the level of malfeasance and extraordinary ineptitude displayed by the four banks cited above hardly can amount to a passing grade.

Non-drones are not immune to mistakes themselves. Apple's board thought it could live without Steve Jobs; turns out just the opposite was true. Home Depot's directors immensely overindulged CEO Robert Nardelli before lowering the boom on him. Despite repeated calls for his resignation and a truly dismal record—think Vista operating system, the Zune MP3 player, and a moribund share price—Steve Ballmer continues to hold down the top job at Microsoft.[143]

But boards in which equity owners still exert a meaningful influence are much less interested in the window dressing. Again, to scan the top six by market cap, Apple's eight-person board includes one person with, by now, very tenuous Washington connections: Al Gore. Microsoft (9-member board), Google (10 members), Oracle (12 members), and Berkshire Hathaway (also 12 members, with a median age north of 70) are heavy with CEOs and even some cross-pollination (Bill Gates serves as board chairman at Microsoft as well as a Berkshire Hathaway director), but these four masters of the economic universe don't have a single ex-political figure among them. Walmart—the largest of the top six non-drone boards—does have a drone-like 17 directors but the only person on it with significant Washington experience is Aida Alvarez, former administrator of the generally low profile Small Business Administration.[144]

Two other distinctions between drone and non-drone boards bear mention:

Number one: asymmetric power. As noted earlier, drone CEOs are nearly 50 percent more likely to serve as board chairman as well. That increases almost exponentially their capacity to name their own boards, but the imbalance of power doesn't stop there. Drones are also more likely to have active CEOs—and retired CEOs—on their compensation committees, and CEOs have a vested interest in upping each other's antes since compensation standards within the broad CEO market are being tweaked with every new package awarded. (Imagine, for example, if NFL quarterbacks were able not just to vote on the salary packages awarded fellow quarterbacks but to head up the committees that set the figures.) Drone directors do occasionally call their CEOs to task, but even then the landing is soft. Witness the Citigroup board, which in October 2012 forced the resignation of Vikram Pandit after five years in the top slot—and then awarded him severance pay of $15.5 million, basically for failing at the job he had been hired to perform.[145]

Item two: skin in the game. Drone and non-drone directors are compensated just about equally for board service: an average of $237,586 to $232,295 annually, for the 500 companies we studied. (The extreme outlier here is Berkshire Hathaway, which pays its directors $900 per meeting, plus expenses—or $300 if they attend by phone.) When it comes to skin in the game, though, it's no contest. Drone board members on average have a stake of about $1.2 million in the companies they direct—roughly five times their average annual compensation for serving as a board member. Non-drone directors have a stake of almost $2.5 million, ten times annual compensation. Mitigation abounds. Drones tend toward commodity companies and establishment directors; non-drones toward nascent industry sectors and roll-the-dice entrepreneurs. But when your reward stands to be greater by not rocking the boat than by trying to pushing it forward into new waters, the status quo has a powerful leg up.[146]

The test of a board isn't its architecture, its reach, its power, or its clout—all that's the parsley on the fish. The test of a board is how the company that directors are supposedly overseeing on behalf of shareholders behaves and performs. On both fronts, drone boards are failing miserably.

Drone Behavior: Low Taxes, Throwaway Workers, Large Fines & Settlements

- Corporate drones are far more likely than non-drones to avoid taxes significantly or altogether. Of the 30 S&P 500 companies identified by Citizens for Tax Justice as having paid no U.S. federal taxes from 2008 to 2010, two thirds were drones. Twenty-six of these companies were able to avoid paying taxes in 2011 as well, including GE, even though it was among the 20 most profitable companies in America that year.

- Corporate drones, on average, laid off nearly 50 percent more workers for the same reporting period.

- Corporate drones are twice as likely as non-drones to have frozen or eliminated pension plans since 2005.

- In terms of regulatory and related fines and settlements paid over the past 20 years, the drones were more than twice as likely to have made such payments, and account for almost 85 percent of the total fines and settlements assessed and paid over the last two decades, more than $80 billion in all.[147]

How does GE manage to pay essentially no corporate U.S. taxes on its vast profits? The best explanation might be the most obvious: GE has the largest tax department in the world. But if GE's profitability is dependent upon zero taxes, and it well might be, isn't it possible that CEO Jeffrey Immelt has the wrong business plan? When so much of an enterprise's energy goes to avoidance, innovation can't help but suffer.

In the same vein, what can one reasonably deduce from the fact that major pharmaceutical firms are in a state of almost constant negotiation and expensive settlements with the FDA and other federal agencies? Again, the best answer might be the most obvious: These firms have a business plan based on fines and the externalization of arguably criminal activity as legitimate sales expenses.

Bloomberg News's David Evans caught the spirit of the worst of Big Pharma's many offenders—Pfizer, the industry's alpha wolf—in a 2010 article that begins thus:

> *Prosecutor Michael Loucks remembers clearly when attorneys for Pfizer, the world's largest drug company, looked across the table and promised it wouldn't break the law again.*
>
> *It was January 2004, and the lawyers were negotiating in a conference room on the ninth floor of the federal courthouse in Boston, where Loucks was head of the health care fraud unit of the U.S. Attorney's Office. One of Pfizer's units had been pushing doctors to prescribe an epilepsy drug called Neurontin for uses the Food and Drug Administration had never approved.*
>
> *In the agreement the lawyers eventually hammered out, the Pfizer unit, Warner-Lambert, pleaded guilty to two felony counts of marketing a drug for unapproved uses. New York-based Pfizer agreed to pay $430 million in criminal fines and civil penalties, and the company's lawyers assured Loucks and three other prosecutors that Pfizer and its units would stop promoting drugs for unauthorized purposes.*
>
> *What Loucks, who was acting U.S. attorney in Boston until November, didn't know until years later was that Pfizer managers were breaking that pledge not to practice off-label marketing even before the ink was dry on their plea.*[148]

And so it has gone continuously for Pfizer and other pharma

drone-firms in the years since: a torrent of penalties, many in the billion-dollar range, many for what any reasonable panel of citizens would consider criminal malfeasance of duty. Add in the energy drones with their toxic spills, the utility drones with their non-complying coal plants, the drone banks we were just looking at (sub-prime, etc.), and the specific social costs of "un-owned," CEO-controlled corporations mount ever moon-ward.

All corporations, of course, are susceptible to this. All humans yield to temptation occasionally, and sometimes more. But drones show a unique capacity in this regard, in part for reasons already mentioned: regal CEOs; go-along, see-no-evil boards. Since 1989, 46 percent of drone firms have paid fines and settlements vs. 24 percent of non-drones. For drones, the average fine or settlement paid per company has been $664 million vs. $265 million for non-drones. Stretch that math out and you come to a truly horrible distinction between drone and non-drone corporations. The former have shelled out almost $82 billion in penalties of all sorts; the latter, just shy of $15 billion, i.e., less than a fifth.[149]

And the bleeding doesn't stop there. Between November 2008 and March 2010, 38 percent of drones laid off workers, vs. 30 percent of non-drones. Average layoff for companies for drones was 3,633 workers, for non-drones 2,351. By paying corporate taxes at a significantly lower rate than their non-drone peers, drones also contributed far less to cushioning the blow for those who got the ax.[150]

Since 2005, 29 drones (vs.14 non-drones) have also frozen or eliminated pension plans for their employees, including some of the most gilt-edged names in business: 3M, Alcoa, CIGNA, du Pont, GE, IBM, Kimberly-Clark, Kraft, State Street, Sunoco, SunTrust Banks, Verizon, and Walt Disney, to just skim the cream off the top. In all, nearly 85,000 pension plans have vanished for American workers since 1985, mostly replaced by 401(k) plans with a median value, as of 2011, of less than $18,000. A crisis of retiree destitution waits just around the corner, yet another rotten fruit of externalization.[151]

Finally, too, there's the unavoidable issue of exactly whose pocket is being picked when, say, an HSBC bank is hit with nearly

$2 billion in penalties, as it recently was for laundering Mexican drug cartel money, executing 25,000 illegal Iranian bank transactions in a single month, and helping Saudi banks funnel money to terrorist groups like al Qaeda. The headlines imply HSBC itself is paying the penalty, as is Barclay's in its $450 million settlement for reporting false rates, or UBS in its expected $1 billion settlement for interest rate manipulation. But HSBC, Barclays, and UBS are legal entities owned by their shareholders. The flesh-and-blood possessors of this equity ultimately absorb the brunt of such fines and penalties, as do customers of all sorts, in higher fees, etc. And the price to be paid by those who actually sanctioned these mostly incontestably criminal activities, or ignored them? If the past is prologue in banking as in pharmaceuticals and elsewhere, they are off scot-free.[152]

GE's vast tax department, the machinations required to circumvent regulators and externalize all corporate responsibility to shareholders and the public at large, these things don't come without a cost. They require enormous corporate energy, even considerable outlay. But is the effort worth it in a world in which profit is king and the bottom line the measure of all success? That depends, in large part, on what the bottom line tells us.

Drone Performance: Far Behind the Competition

- Most important, on average, over the period 2007-present, the 269 corporate drones that comprise a majority of the current S&P 500 *dramatically under-performed their non-drone counterparts in terms of investment returns to shareholders.*

However one parses the numbers, the results come out the same. Total shareholder return for non-drones in 2011, the last year for which full figures are available, was 6.59 percent vs. 4.93 percent for drones, a third greater. Go back to the three years immediately after the financial collapse, 2009-2011 when stock prices were struggling to return to pre-crisis values, and the margin is less but still statistically meaningful: 20 percent. Stretch back to five years, and the total shareholder return for non-drones exceeds that of drones by 23 percent.[153]

These should be worrisome figures for investors, but they are deeply troubling for society as well. The world trends toward corporate-drone status for all the reasons we have looked at throughout this book—algorithms; index trading; ascendant CEOs; the breaking of the old atom of ownership; courts, politicians, and regulators captured by corporate wealth; academics, the chattering classes, the best and brightest college graduates drawn in, too.

Simultaneously, corporate ownership devolves to six managers—BlackRock, State Street, Fidelity, Vanguard, Northern Trust, and Mellon—who are generally passive in their oversight (BlackRock, as we'll see, is emerging as the exception) and deeply conflicted by massive cross-ownership within particular sectors. State Street, for example, is the largest single institutional shareholder in six of the top sixteen defense contractors. How does it exercise ownership influence over Lockheed Martin, say, without affecting its 4 percent stake in L-3 Communications? Answer: It doesn't, which more and more leaves corporate control even in something as important as armaments up to a handful of manager-kings willing to externalize almost anything in the name of profit (their own included) when the overwhelming evidence shows that a laser-like focus on profit (their own included) produces inferior returns.[154]

The logical extension of this is a world in which corporations become ever more rogue and ever less efficient, while their residual wealth flows mostly to the very few keepers who hold the keys to their ever-diminishing treasuries. This is not a sustainable strategy for successfully competing in the dog-eat-dog global economy that CEOs and their mouthpieces (BRT, U.S. Chamber of Commerce, and the like) frequently cite to justify their drone-like behavior. Nor can even the most powerful drone externalize everything forever. There is always a day of reckoning. The only variables are when, where, what, and how.

How have we gotten to this point? By many routes, but primarily by making the same mistake as a society that the U.S. Supreme Court made legally when it enshrined corporate personhood in its *Citizens United* decision: assuming that corporate values and goals and human values and goals are ultimately one and the same. They are not.

To cite only the most obvious examples:

Corporations favor *power applied top-down*, they thrive on *competition*, and they tend toward *hegemony*. Human goals are, or should include, *fairness, cooperation*, and a *pluralism* of backgrounds, perspectives, skills, and interest groups.

Corporations are *rule driven*. They *measure accountability* via cost-benefit calculations. Corporations *externalize* their costs and *deplete resources* in the pursuit of profit. In the end, they are judged by the marketplace, answer to their stakeholders, and do everything they can to avoid personal responsibility for their failures. Humans are, or again should be, *principle driven*. We are at our best when we measure accountability *holistically*, not only in dollars and cents but in the total impact of our functioning on the quality of life, the values we hold dear, and the rules we live by. Humans are accountable ultimately to *society as a whole*.

Finally, in terms of *ethics*, corporations are built around efficiency, limited liability, and a winner-takes-all mentality—measured across the short term and rewarded in material ways, whether compensation, advancement, title, etc. We humans are in it for the long haul, not just for ourselves but for our children's children's children. In weighing right and wrong, we need to go beyond material rewards to the emotional and spiritual underpinnings of our humanity. In the drone vocabulary, words like "sympathy," "empathy," "dignity," and "respect" barely exist. In the human vocabulary, they are integral to ethics, to the life well led. Humans don't have limited liability. We have *unlimited responsibility*, including unlimited responsibility for the corporations that function, or dysfunction, in our name.

By failing to take into account these profound differences between drone ethics and human ones, the Supreme Court majority in *Citizens United* delivered not only a surpassingly odd verdict but a superlatively undemocratic one. The great authors of the U.S. Constitution might have talked about God-given rights, but their concern was always with what was best for the flesh-and-blood beings who would be existing within the governmental system the framers set out to create. Granting drone corporations, in effect, unlimited hegemony changes the ethical language within which and through which our government functions and our citizens live. America today is a different country than the one of our historical myths and, for most of us, the one of our aspirations. And the hour for fighting back is extraordinarily late.

> *Question: Is anyone really accountable for the behavior and results of corporations in America today?*

****

7.

Responsibility, Accountability, and Shame

There is no such thing to my mind . . . as an innocent stockholder.
He may be innocent in fact, but socially he cannot be held
innocent. He accepts the benefits of the system. It is his business
and his obligation to see that those who represent him carry out a
policy which is consistent with the public welfare.

— Louis Brandeis

They were still burying schoolchildren in Newtown, Connecticut, when the private equity firm Cerberus Capital Management announced that it would be selling the Freedom Group, manufacturer of the .223 Bushmaster assault rifle used to mow down six adults and 20 first-graders at Sandy Hook Elementary School.

Cerberus, whose leadership team includes former Vice President Dan Quayle and former Business Roundtable Chairman and U.S. Treasury Secretary John Snow, had purchased Bushmaster in 2006. The company was later merged with other arms manufacturers to create the Freedom Group, which the firm's website describes as "the world's leading innovator, designer, manufacturer and marketer of firearms, ammunition and related products for the hunting, shooting sports, law enforcement and military markets."[155]

Cerberus left little doubt that the decision to sell "the world's leading innovator, etc." had less to do with the massacre itself than with market conditions in its aftermath: "It is apparent that the Sandy Hook tragedy was a watershed event that has raised the national debate on gun control to an unprecedented level," as the press release put it.[156] But unmentioned in that communiqué was another, far more powerful precipitating event: a statement from the super-size California State Teachers' Retirement System, or CalSTRS, that it was reviewing its investment in Cerberus specifically because of its holding in the Freedom Group. And underlying the importance of that was a simple hard fact: As of March 2012, CalSTRS had over $750 million invested with Cerberus, and commitments for much more.[157]

The moral: Sympathy walks; money talks.

We've seen this before, of course, if never quite so starkly, washed in the blood of so many little innocents. Events specific or, more often, general lead to public outrage; the rage focuses on specific industry groups, perhaps on specific products and stocks; and the dormant giants of investing are finally stirred to action, or perhaps not. Over the last 40 years, campaigns against tobacco products, cluster bombs, and apartheid in South Africa have all led to major institutional divestitures of holdings in related companies, as well as to major institutional resistance.

As I write, a Harvard group calling itself Students for a Just and Stable Future is pressuring the Harvard Corporation—which oversees the university's endowment, with $30 billion-plus in assets—to divest itself of holdings in fossil-fuel producers. After refusing multiple times to meet with the student group, Harvard president Drew Gilpin Faust, *ex officio* head of the Corporation, announced the creation of a donor alternative—a "social-choice fund" within the endowment that will "take special account of social responsibility considerations." This builds on the work of the Coalition for Responsible Investment at Harvard (I'm on the Board of Advisors) and might even represent the beginning of a trend. The Harvard Management Company has since appointed a new Vice President of Sustainable Investment to monitor environmental, social, and governance issues as they relate to the endowment. But why should this be so hard? Harvard, one hopes, is ultimately about bettering the world. To support with its endowment investments in corporations and business models that have exactly the opposite effect is a fundamental contradiction. And as we saw in the last chapter, it is also fundamentally bad investment practice.[158]

The struggle, in short, goes on—a minuet between specific stimuli (a schoolhouse slaughter, Hurricane Sandy, global warming) and carefully calibrated and well-publicized institutional responses

110

(divestiture, social-choice funds, and the like). But here's the real point I wish to make out of all this: In Corporate America today, the stimuli are constant, omnipresent, insufficiently noted, and collectively (if not individually) truly frightening; and the institutional responses continue to be largely massive indifference.

Let me be clear: Nothing, *absolutely nothing* can touch the sheer awfulness of what happened on December 14, 2012, at Sandy Hook Elementary School. No threat to the well-being of the planet and all the people living on it might be greater than the one Harvard students are now protesting. Global warming, greenhouse gases— they're the 800-million-pound gorilla in everyone's closet today. But simultaneously, the social fabric of America and our foundational democratic system are being willfully shredded by far more than a handful of America's leading corporations. This bears more than passing notice as well.

Consider the record we've looked at in this book thus far: a political system awash in corporate cash, regulators effectively captured by corporate interests, "intellectuals" bought off by corporate largess, tax-protected think tanks that "think" only in lockstep with their corporate financiers, CEOs pillaging their own treasuries, an ever-expanding chasm between average and executive pay, corporate boards with the backbone of jellyfish.

And look at the results—entirely predictable—of this greed unchecked and run amok. The 269 S&P 500 firms where passive ownership is the rule (what I term drone corporations) have accounted for $80 billion in fines and settlements over the past two decades, 85 percent of the value of all fines and settlements assessed against all S&P 500 firms during that time.[159] Led two-to-one by the drones, almost 85,000 pension plans have simply disappeared since 1985, gone *poof* into the night, replaced by 401(k) accounts that virtually guarantee a penurious old age while the profits to be reaped from such an abrogation of duty flow (among other places) to the golden parachutes of executives already paid at a scale that would have pleased a Medici.[160] Meanwhile, total shareholder return for the 226 S&P 500 companies with more active, more vested ownership has exceeded that of the drone corporations by a collective 23 percent over the last five years.[161] Whether your criterion is the broad public good (stopping corporations from externalizing all risk obligations to shareholders, customers, and society), the narrower public benefit of stopping corporations from externalizing their worker obligations to the workers themselves, or the ancient fiduciary obligation of securing the best returns for those who entrust their savings to you, corporate America today is increasingly an unchecked menace. Yet where are the voices in protest of all this—not on the street, not in the Occupy Movement, but among the Great and Good, in the boardrooms of our largest and most prestigious institutional investors, pension funds, and endowments, where the decisions are made that ultimately fund this orgy of corporate malfeasance and misbehavior. That's the issue we take up in this chapter.

Who Is Responsible?

This is murky territory, legally and morally. If I have strong reason to believe that my neighbor beats his wife—I hear her screams, I hear the children crying, I hear the occasional crunch of fist on flesh and bone—am I responsible for reporting the abuse to authorities before a black eye becomes a concussion becomes inner-cranial bleeding becomes death? Religion tells us to do unto others as we would have them do unto ourselves, and presumably most of us, were we in the wife's situation above, would welcome intervention. But not all abuse victims do, for whatever convoluted reasons, and maybe we're in fact hearing a TV show or a DVD or a video game so demented that we can barely fathom why anyone would be playing it. Maybe, too, if I report my neighbor and his wife refuses to corroborate my concerns, he'll turn his rage on me. These decisions are never as easy in practice as they are on paper.

So it is with perhaps 99 percent of those Americans entitled to call themselves shareholders. They cannot claim to be entirely innocent of the abuses committed in their name, with their equity, by those who manage the corporations they have invested in. As Louis Brandeis put it, they have accepted the benefits of the system—dividends, rising (one hopes) share value, etc.—and thus they have an obligation to see that the public welfare is being served by the actions of these manager-kings. But practically speaking, not one shareholder in ten million has any idea how far and wide his investments are spread or any capacity whatsoever to influence events at those corporations or even the means to do so, given the meaninglessness of proxy voting and the ruinous expense of trying to insert oneself and one's convictions into the proxy process. So, yes, there *are* no innocent shareholders, but this is an instance where lack of innocence doesn't automatically equate to its opposite: guilt.

The same can't be said of the fewer than one percent of Americans who, in essence, direct the flow of the vast percentage of the nation's wealth: pension-fund managers and other trustees; vast university endowments (Harvard most prominent among them); the great private charities (The Bill and Melinda Gates Foundation); the top executives of leading mutual fund purveyors such as the Vanguard Group, with over $1.6 trillion under management (equal to roughly the gross domestic product of Mexico); and fabulously wealthy investment houses such as Boston's State Street Corporation with over $23 trillion under custody and administration (one-and-a-half times the GDP of the United States).[162]

Here, within this leadership class of money—the Great and Good of investing—there are not and cannot be any innocents. Everyone knows intimately the pattern of money in politics, how lobbying and the "revolving door" effectively neuter corporate oversight. They might find the present situation acceptable in terms of their own self-interest. They might even recite to themselves nightly the same 30-year-old mantra that the Supreme Court invoked in its *Citizens United* decision—that independent directors, government regulators, public opinion, and even the marketplace, guarantee that CEOs and the corporations they direct will be accountable. But those same 30 years have provided continuing, uninterrupted, and ever-accelerating proof that in the United States today there exists no meaningful limit to corporate power within the state, and the Great and Good of investing are far, far too smart to have missed that fact.

CEO pay, of and by itself, is full testimony to the absence of any viable system of checks and balances within the corporate framework. The elimination of pensions for private sector employees over the last decade is social engineering practiced by profit-seeking corporations. Citigroup's not being nationalized is compelling tribute to the power of lobbyists, and the many, many compromises required to secure the passage of Obamacare illustrate that national policy can be implemented only within the framework of corporate interest.

American policy today is informed not by the health of individual citizens but by the priorities of corporate well-being. Witness the billions spent in the wake of the 2008 financial collapse for bailouts, while not one cent went for mortgage relief. The responsibility of government today is conceived as assuring a corporate-friendly environment with no particular resource allocation to individual citizens. (War itself has become a profit center for favored corporations, while the risks of fighting are externalized to the young men and women on the front lines and the costs drive up the public debt.) Government has ceased having a human connection. Its energies flow to impersonal imperatives, corporate performance.

At some level, most of society knows this. At an intimate level, the Great and Good of investing do, yet rather than challenge the conventional wisdom, they take refuge in tired nostrums: With respect to marketable securities, for example, there lingers the traditional attitude that the holder always has the choice of "sale" if she doesn't approve of the product. For their part, institutional investors like to proclaim that they do not buy stock with the intention of being involved in the governance of the company. It all begins to resemble a racetrack where none of the horse owners will take on responsibility for assuring that the "nags aren't doped." No one sane would bet at such a track—or no one who did not have inside knowledge of which horses are in fact doped—and yet we accept stock markets in which there is only illusory responsibility for the integrity of the goods traded.

Perhaps all this denial is just human nature, but it's an end game nonetheless. And when the party does shut down, there's going to be hell to pay.

Who Should Be Held Accountable?

114

In a 2010 interview with my friend and frequent collaborator Nell Minow, Warren Buffett addressed the issue of corporate behavior thus: "If you had the top five institutional investors, and when they saw something outrageous the five of them spoke together . . . the world would change."[163] Buffett was speaking particularly about boards at the time, and he cautioned against pontificating on frivolous matters, but his comment still gets to an essential truth about corporations: They *do* have owners, and owners are capable, *if they so choose* and *if they have sufficient ownership stakes*, of holding corporations and their manager-kings accountable for their behavior.

Pfizer, as we saw in the last chapter, is both an industry leader in corporate malfeasance and the tenth largest corporate drone in the S&P 500. No single entity owns or controls as much as 5 percent of Pfizer's 7.5 billion outstanding shares. Its atom of ownership, to return once more to Justice Brandeis, has been definitively broken. But two institutional investors alone own or control nearly 8.5 percent of Pfizer: Vanguard, with 325.51 million shares, and State Street with 316.54 million. Add in the next three biggest holders of Pfizer stock—Wellington Management (167.07 million shares), T. Rowe Price (133.21 million), and Franklin Resources (113.6 million)—and suddenly you have five institutional owners who together have a 14 percent stake in the company, enough to command the attention of even the most arrogant—or tone-deaf—CEO.[164]

What would happen if these five institutional owners began to question the long-term viability of a business plan that calls for externalizing all risk to Pfizer's customers and society as a whole—or the effectiveness of a board of directors that seems content to endorse a business plan built on borderline criminal activity? (The Pfizer board, it should be noted, does not have a great long-term track record: In 2006, the board forced out then CEO Henry McKinnell after Pfizer's had lost 40 percent of its market-cap value during his five-year watch, then rewarded McKinnell with a secret pension package worth $5.9 million a year, or—incredibly—more if he were to remarry.) At the least, shouldn't these Big Five Pfizer investors be concerned that total shareholder returns appear to be significantly higher at firms with more active ownership?[165]

And if they are not concerned about a business plan that routinely puts customers at risk or a mode of passive ownership that appears to work against shareholder interests, shouldn't Pfizer's Big Five investors themselves be called to account? Are sins of omission less culpable than sins of commission?

The same set of questions could easily be asked about BP, a serial offender of the environment. It shares three of the same top five owners as Pfizer: Wellington, State Street, and Franklin Resources. Is their obligation here any less? Look at the Texas City refinery explosion of 2005. Look at the Deepwater Horizon explosion of 2010. Count the dead and injured workers, the ongoing damage to the Gulf and its wetlands. The evidence that BP simply skimped on safety measures in both instances would appear to be compelling. The billions in fines the company has agreed to pay provide their own form of acknowledgement, but the money in question provides no promise that BP won't be back to business as usual until the next explosion, the next environmental disaster. Indeed, its status as a serial offender argues exactly the opposite. If the corporation has no conscience of its own—if its "personhood" is that of a cold-blooded profit machine— then is it the obligation of BP's leading institutional investors to begin to provide one? Or to insist on truly independent voices in the BP board room?[166]

IBM presents a more nuanced instance of the same basic set of queries. Big Blue deservedly has many admirers, but IBM also led the way in gutting corporate pension plans and gave encouragement to (and cover for) many lesser firms that followed suit.[167] In the narrow horizon, this undoubtedly has worked to IBM's advantage and to the advantage of corporate America generally, but over the longer sweep, what are the implications for an economy ever more dragged down by an aging population whose 401(k) plans are nowhere sufficient to its needs? And have IBM's top five owners—in reverse order, J.P Morgan Chase, Wellington, Vanguard, State Street, and Warren Buffett's Berkshire Hathaway—even bothered to think about these matters, much less address them to a management that seems so proud of ridding itself of a pension system that once helped stabilize the middle class even unto (to get Biblical) its golden years?

The great foundations would seem to have a clearer mandate to do good, or at least to do no harm, and indeed the very greatest of them all in terms of wealth, The Bill and Melinda Gates Foundation, explicitly tackles this issue on its website:

Bill and Melinda do guide the managers of the foundation's endowment in voting proxies consistent with the principles of good governance and good management. When instructing the investment managers, Bill and Melinda also consider other issues beyond corporate profits, including the values that drive the foundation's work. They have defined areas in which the endowment will not invest, such as companies whose profit model is centrally tied to corporate activity that they find egregious. This is why the endowment does not invest in tobacco stocks...[168]

It's a noble statement, in many ways a model for other foundations, and there's no question that Bill and Melinda Gates through their foundation do a world of good. Yet as of September 2012, the Gates Foundation's eighth largest holding was in ExxonMobil, a company whose annual meetings have all the democratic trappings of a Stalin-era gathering of the Soviet People's Congress. As of that same date, the foundation also held 7.13 million shares of the aforementioned BP, about which enough has already been written.[169] Is pressure coming from this corner of the Great and Good to open proxy access to ExxonMobil, or to find a business plan for BP that doesn't rely on externalizing environmental risk and safety? One is hard pressed to have faith in either possibility.

Public employee pension funds make even the Gates Foundation look puny by comparison. CalPERS, the California Public Employees' fund, has somewhere over $220 billion under management.[170] New York State, New York City, Florida, and Texas teachers' funds all top $100 billion.[171] As the California State Teachers' Retirement fund (circa $140 billion) showed so effectively in the wake of the Newtown massacre, corporations listen when so much money speaks. But for CalSTRS, Newtown was a specific, compelling case that almost demanded action. Teachers and students had been slaughtered. A pension fund created to serve educators should not have trouble stirring itself to action in such a circumstance.[172]

Imagine, though, if that same pressure were consistently applied to rationalizing CEO pay, to ending the Compensation Committee buddy system, to regulatory compliance, to scaling back the off-shoring of revenues, to humanizing these drone-like profit monsters we call corporations. Society might actually be improved. The energy expended to externalize all obligations might flow instead to improving the bottom line. This is, after all, the solemn fiduciary duty of those who are investing these pension funds. That duty simply cannot be fulfilled through silence, through inaction, and yet that is the modus operandi of far too many pension fund managers and executives: See no evil, hear no evil, speak no evil. At some point, a failure to recognize evil becomes evil itself.

Like foundations and public employee pension funds, university endowments would seem to have a unique role in society. They are repositories of vast wealth: As of June 2011, the top five university endowments—Harvard, Yale, Princeton, the University of Texas, and Stanford, in order—totaled a collective $102 billion.[173] They have constituencies that are far more alert than the population as a whole to issues such as global warming, regulatory abuse, and a rapidly shrinking middle class. And yet—witness Harvard and the unwillingness of its endowment officials to directly deal with Students for a Just and Stable Future—their endowments often seem 100 percent committed to profit, minimally interested in how it is achieved, and as willing as anywhere else in the private sector to pay a king's ransom to those entrusted with the care of their billions.

Harvard Management Company's Jane Mendillo earned total compensation of $4.75 million in 2011 for directing the university's $30 billion-plus in investments. Would it have killed her to take half a day to explain to a group of undergraduates concerned over Harvard's carbon footprint why the university owned nearly a million shares of Sunoco as of September 30, 2012? If Yale students were to approach president Richard Levin with concerns that 5.7 percent of that university's endowment was tied up in shares of Approach Resources, a Texas-based producer of oil and natural gas, would Yale's chief endowment investor officer, David Swensen ($3.8 million in total compensation in 2011), react any differently? Again, it's hard to have faith in such a possible outcome.[174]

And if it is unrealistic to expect much more from the Great and Good of Investing at the Best and Brightest of American institutions, then what really are the prospects of reversing a trend that seems to be inexorably yielding power to corporate interests intent on a narrow agenda built entirely around their own wants and needs?

Two maxims occur to me at this point. The first is the old rhyme generally attributed to George Herbert about compounding circumstances:

For want of a nail the shoe was lost.
For want of a shoe the horse was lost.
For want of a horse the rider was lost.
For want of a rider the message was lost.
For want of a message the battle was lost.
For want of a battle the kingdom was lost.
And all for the want of a horseshoe nail.

The second is a popular adaptation of a phrase that probably dates back to the pre-Christian Jewish sage Hillel the Elder: "If not me, who? If not now, when?"

Somewhere—nail, shoe, horse, rider, message, battle—the kingdom of that great economic engine known as democratic capitalism has been all but lost. Who will stand up to reclaim it? When?

Who Can Make a Difference?

Through the conveniently rosy lenses of the Supreme Court majority in *Citizens United*, the answer is easy: Everyone! Individual shareholders by their vigilant attention and carefully considered proxy votes. Fund managers by their close parsing of the public records of political contributions and return on investments, and the more private and often intuitive ones of the effectiveness of governance

119

at the corporations toward which they direct their funds' resources. Even the media and online watchdogs, by bringing to public attention the wretched excesses and imperial ambitions of so many corporate manager-kings.

In the world in which meaningful change actually occurs, though, those who can make a true and lasting difference—who can lead the charge, who can raise the flag that others follows—are perilously few: not the funds per se, not their hired managers, however handsomely they are rewarded, but the trustees who stand behind them and are both legal owners of the entities and moral owners of their actions. They, the trustees, have ultimate power, and thus they have ultimate responsibility and accountability. By my count, they are 24 in number, the tip of the tip of the tip of the spear in defense of truly democratic capitalism. I list them below.

Bill and Melinda Gates Foundation
Bill Gates
Melinda Gates
Warren Buffett

Ford Foundation
Chair – Irene Hirano Inouye
President – Luis A. Ubiñas

J. Paul Getty Trust
Chairman – Mark S. Siegel
President and CEO – James Cuno

Robert Wood Johnson Foundation
Chairman – Thomas H. Kean
President and CEO – Risa Lavizzo-Mourey

William and Flora Hewlett Foundation
Chairman – Walter B. Hewlett
President – Larry Kramer

David and Lucille Packard Foundation
Chair – Susan Packard Orr

President – Julie E. Packard

Harvard Corporation – President and Fellows
Senior Fellow – Robert D. Reischauer
President – Drew Gilpin Faust

Yale Corporation
Senior Fellow – Edward Perry Bass
President – Richard C. Levin

Princeton – Board of Trustees
Chair – Kathryn A. Hall
President – Shirley M. Tilghman

Stanford – Board of Trustees
Chairman – Steven Denning
President – John L. Hennessy

University of Texas System – Board of Regents
Chair – Wm. Eugene "Gene" Powell

MIT Corporation
Chairman – John S. Reed
President – L. Rafael Reif

Collectively, these leaders control approximately $200 billion of endowment assets, a king's ransom, but happily, they do not have to do the whole job themselves.[175] Other conspicuously committed and enormously wealthy institutions have set a high standard of stewardship. Among them: the Government Pension Fund Global-Norway with $575 billion; the Public Employees' Retirement System of California with $220 billion and the California State Teachers' Fund with $140 billion, and Ontario Teachers' Pension Plan with $115 billion.[176] Laurence Fink, CEO of BlackRock, the largest money manager in the world with in excess of $3.5 trillion, has also committed his organization to act as a responsible owner and has appointed Michele Edkins, one of the world's leading corporate professionals, to be head of global governance.[177]

A Minimum Ownership Agenda

What might one reasonably expect from the Great and Good of Investing — the two dozen vital trustees listed earlier plus the proven stewards mentioned just above? Allow me to suggest two baseline commitments — momentum changers, if not game changers, and quite possibly both:

- Requiring as a *condition of investment* (new or continuing) corporate management to commit to investigating, formulating, and implementing an accounting system that holistically represents the full impact of corporate functioning on society. Externalized costs don't disappear from society, as I've suggested throughout this book; they are shunted on to other entities — governments, foundations, charities, workers, society generally. Legitimate bookkeeping demands recognizing and incorporating this reality into every corporate P&L statement.

- Requiring as a *condition of investment* (new or continuing) that corporate management disclose publicly and seek shareholder approval for all politically motivated lobbying and contributions. These hidden costs to society don't disappear either — just the opposite.

Consider the case of Amgen, the world's largest biotech company. Buried in the "fiscal cliff" legislation that passed Congress at the end of 2012 was a stealth provision that delayed by two years price restraints on an Amgen drug aimed at kidney dialysis patients. Expected to cost Medicare (which is to say American taxpayers) on the order of half a billion dollars, this eleventh-hour addition to the legislation was the collective work of 74 paid Amgen lobbyists in the nation's Capital and the company's long-time financial support for, among others, Senate Minority Leader Mitch McConnell and Senate Finance Committee stalwarts Max Baucus and Orrin Hatch. Perhaps Amgen shareholders would have happily approved such a vast expenditure of company funds to such a self-interested end had they

122

known about it and had the opportunity to vote on same, but they did not, and ignorance is not and never has been moral bliss.[178]

What Is Shame?

Shame, my friend Donald Munro has written, "is not embarrassment, and it is not guilt." Rather, shame "concerns diminished self worth, based in part on knowledge that others know that one has broken a rule."[179] The precondition for great shame, then, is to have committed a great and public transgression, and here is one of the worst I can conceive of: to have known vast harm was being done and to have had the power, standing, and resources to intervene, and yet to have failed to act. That is a shame not easily overcome, for the individual or for the society that allowed it to happen.

As Edith Hamilton once wrote, in the quote that opens this book:

When the freedom they wished for most was freedom from responsibility, then Athens ceased to be free and was never free again.

****

8.
The Ownership Imperative

I'm not a conventionally religious man, but my father, Gardner Monks, was an Episcopal priest, and these many decades later I still sometimes find myself framing issues in the words of the hymns that were so much a part of my youth. So it is with the issue that has inspired this book: the corporate capture of America's wealth and polity.

The hymn in question first appeared as a poem in the *Boston Courier* of December 11, 1845. The poet, James Russell Lowell, would go on to become editor of the *Atlantic Monthly*, a noted Harvard professor, U.S. Ambassador to Spain and Great Britain, and (ironically) a leading progenitor of the Brahmin culture that drove me from Boston more than forty years ago.

Lowell's purpose in putting pen to paper on this occasion was to rally opposition to an American war with Mexico. In that, he failed— President Polk asked Congress to declare war exactly five months after Lowell's poem was published, and Congress obliged two days later— but Lowell's opening lines remain a stirring call to action:

Once to every man and nation, comes the moment to decide,
In the strife of truth with falsehood, for the good or evil side;
Some great cause, some great decision, offering each the
bloom or blight, And the choice goes by forever, 'twixt that
darkness and that light.[180]

Have we reached such a tipping point, one of those crucial moments in history to decide between two kinds of America: one, a corporatist state, dominated and informed by corporate wants and needs; the other, a government and a nation of the people, by the people, and for the people? I think we have.

Capture has occurred—we know that. Corporate governance is a chimera at best, a fraud at worst; corporate ownership is dispersed to the point of dilution; corporate agendas are increasingly national agendas. We know, too, that drone corporations are materially different than owned ones. They behave worse. Their CEOs have their hands deeper in the corporate till. They externalize more of their obligations and yield lower total shareholder returns than their "owned" counterparts. Far more troubling, they represent the future toward which all corporations are tending. The more mature an enterprise becomes, the more it assumes drone-like characteristics and becomes driven by an ethic of profit at any cost to society.

Finally, we know that the conventional alleged restraints on corporate power are not only ineffective but also provide cover for an ever-tightening grip on the national jugular—a way to avoid looking squarely at what is, in fact, happening before our very eyes.

Yes, a corporation is a creature of law. It has no common-law right to exist. In theory, a domicile state can withdraw a corporation charter as punishment for bad behavior, but the realities of taxation and competition with other states have rendered this remedy all but meaningless. Rather than hold to the high ground, states find themselves racing to the bottom to accommodate a growing demand for minimal taxes and maximum deregulation, and to counter a constant threat of imminent departure.

The same applies to the race to the bottom between nations. While a sovereign can style a corporation criminal, prosecute its representatives, and assess large fines, it dare not deprive such a wrongdoer of eligibility to conduct normal business except for token suspensions. Globalization and the capacity of corporations to domicile their operations wherever convenient have virtually eliminated any national government's capacity effectively to control corporate functioning. So it is also with antitrust laws and other direct regulatory statutes. Their effectiveness is neutered by the vast asymmetry between the stateless global corporation and the necessarily confined nation-state.

126

In the same vein, "Treasure Islands" have rendered null and void the capacity of domiciles to influence corporate behavior through another traditional tool: taxation. For individuals, tax codes remain a powerful form of social disciplining, even social engineering, but corporations who dislike what tax policies are asking them to do can simply relocate operations and income to someplace like the Cayman Islands, where overhead and infrastructure costs amount to little more than a postal box and a resident representative.

Markets are also thought to discipline corporations, and so they do within the ambit of their particular products, but there is no market in "good governance." Nor is it possible to make a convincing case that good governance can be a win/win situation for shareholders and management, so long as management can direct a disproportionate share of company resources to itself and its protection. Here, again, the asymmetry is simply overwhelming.

Public opinion, industry associations, public interest groups, the standards for lawyers, accountants, and other professionals—none of them has had any appreciable impact on corporate conduct. Nor has a drubbing so thorough been lost on the nation's youth. Over the last two decades, so many of our "best and brightest" students have gone to work as investment bankers, consultants, and more recently, hedge-fund impresarios—a brain-drain away from government that has severely impacted the power to enforce laws. Thus, for example, when Microsoft was first prosecuted for antitrust violations, the Justice Department felt compelled to hire an outside lawyer, the much-celebrated David Boies, to represent the government.[181]

All this perhaps explains why everyone invests so heavily in the Myth of Corporate Governance: It is in everyone's interest to pretend such a thing exists. Yet every bit of evidence shows us that effective control of corporations can be exercised *only from the inside*.

Thus, by default, we end up with the only participant in the corporate constellation who is both independent of management power, motivated by its own financial interest, and competent—in law, in quality of professional advisors, and in cooperation with other shareholders—effectively to control corporate conduct: the largest

127

owners of equity in those corporations and, in particular, the trustees of those largest owners. Their names can be found in the previous chapter.

Why Must They Act Now?

Ten reasons:

- Because for reasons already illuminated, there must be a functioning "owner" in every publicly traded corporation.

- Because the trustees of our leading university and foundation endowments — Bill and Melinda Gates, Warren Buffett, Harvard's Drew Faust, to put names on the most prominent of these positions and people — are thoroughly decent and concerned individuals who have already contributed hugely to human welfare.

- Because corporate capture is beyond question, and because there is no plausible alternative solution to their involvement.

- Because the greed of "unowned" drones is sterile, which in the end, can only create a sterile economy, bereft of any innovation that doesn't serve the ends of self-enrichment.

- Because these trustees have the resources — intellectual, institutional, and financial — to devise the structures through which effective ownership can be expressed.

- Because ownership-based governance provides symmetry between the corporations' global impact and the geographic limits of their sovereign domicile.

- Because, as we'll see soon, the very elements that have done so much to create passive ownership — in particular, index funds and algorithm trading — provide foundational opportunities for an ownership solution.

- Because the full commitment of the most respected institutional investors is essential to the legitimacy and effectiveness of ownership involvement in corporate governance, and because that ownership involvement is the only modality through which capitalist energies can be accommodated with human welfare.

- Because recent events—from the grass-roots Occupy Movement to efforts by BlackRock, the world's largest money manager, to rein in executive pay at a number of firms in its portfolio—suggest that at long last CEOs might have overplayed their hand, and a moment of opportunity is near.[182]

- And because the need is great, the hour late, and the stakes could not be higher, we have indeed reached a precipice beyond which lies the imminent destruction of an economic, political, and social system that has endured for over 200 years. To let that go without a fight would be unconscionable.

Chrystia Freeland captured this last point brilliantly in her book *Plutocrats: The Rise of the New Global Super-Rich and the Fall of Everyone Else* and in an essay based on her book that appeared in the October 14, 2012, "Sunday Review" section of the *New York Times*. Allow me here to boil her argument down to a fine nub:

At every tier of the economic pyramid except the very top, American society is fraying. Many factors are to blame: globalization, technological change, perhaps even culture, in the form of a collapsing work ethic, but public policy in the service of corporate ends and the mostly mega-rich has accelerated all these trends. While executive compensation has soared, the tax burden on the very rich has shrunk to levels that would have been unthinkable a half century ago. (A tax burden, one should add, not materially changed by "fiscal cliff" legislation, given the vast number of loopholes available to the very rich that still exist in the U.S. tax code.) Simultaneously, labor unions have been largely marginalized through a relentless attack by corporate-backed think tanks.

Meanwhile, educational attainment, the historical ladder up for the American middle class, is no longer rising for the population as a whole. The top independent schools, repository for the children of the very rich and well-connected (Barack Obama as well as Mitt Romney), prosper as never before, while public schools starve, and crony capitalism works to assure that whatever the twists and turns of the economic roller-coaster, the top of the pyramid will continue to be served and the bottom further deprived.

Evidence: the bipartisan, $700 billion rescue of Wall Street in 2008. As Freeland notes, "The economists Emmanuel Saez and Thomas Piketty found that 93 percent of the income gains from the 2009-10 recovery went to the top 1 percent of taxpayers. The top 0.01 percent captured 37 percent of these additional earnings, gaining an average of $4.2 million per household." Further evidence: "the tax perks, trade protections and government subsidies that companies and sectors secure for themselves."

All of which should, perhaps, be cause for great celebration by the super rich and powerful, including the very trustees to whom I am here appealing, except they—I am certain—understand what those who cannot stop extracting from the corporate treasury don't and won't: that in every country, in every place, in every time, there has been finally an end to pillage. The only real question is whether that cessation comes through the exercise of responsible leadership or through blood in the streets.

"It is no accident," Freeland writes, "that in America today the gap between the very rich and everyone else is wider than at any time since the Gilded Age. Now, as then, the titans are seeking an even greater political voice to match their economic power. Now, as then, the inevitable danger is that they will confuse their own self-interest with the common good. The irony of the political rise of the plutocrats is that . . . they threaten the system that created them."[183]

False Hopes & Delusions

Before we get to a way out of the maze, we need to look at two "solutions" to corporate capture that have served only to draw us deeper into the labyrinth. The first is "negative investing," whether in the form of divestiture or simply declining to invest in particular companies, either because of the businesses they are in (tobacco, firearms, etc.) or the people they do business with (apartheid), or because of consistently bad corporate behavior.

The impetus behind divestiture is often noble. Sometimes, as with CalSTRS in the wake of the Newtown massacre, a moral imperative demands to be honored. From the outside, too, it's hard to press for much more than jettisoning offensive holdings. The Harvard students demanding the university's endowment rid itself of fossil-fuel-related holdings have few if any other options for expressing their concern over global warming. But for the owners of those stocks—the endowment, not the students—divestiture is tantamount to declaring moral victory, deserting the field of battle, and leaving festering in place whatever was offensive enough to merit the divesting, along with CEOs who frankly don't give a damn who owns the stock as long as someone does.

In the end, nothing changes, or perhaps what changes is not what was hoped for or intended. Nelson Mandela once told me that he had great respect for those companies that continued to do business in apartheid South Africa because (a) they provided employment at a turbulent time for the economy and the nation, and (b) their presence kept up the pressure to reform.

Similarly, refusing to invest in particular companies or industry groups in the first place—hard-core negative investing—is likely to produce a wealth of warm and fuzzy feelings, but too often, doing so is also taken to be a full and effective discharge of ownership responsibilities generally, no matter the holding and no matter its behavior. The tobacco companies and assault-rifle makers you don't invest in won't miss your money, while the manager-kings of the banks and Big Pharma companies where you do park your wealth are only too happy to have you convinced that your ownership duties have already been fulfilled. Worse by far, shirking ownership responsibilities in this way continues to trivialize the efforts of those "owners" who do fight for change on the inside and finally destroys shareholder activism as a legitimating force for corporate power in a democracy.

The second false hope to be dashed here amounts to a personal admission of failure. For four decades I have been preaching the power of shareholder democracy: one share, one vote—nothing more, never anything less. Others obviously have agreed because this is, above all else, the gold standard of the investment business, required for listing on the New York Stock Exchange.

I still believe that in an ideal world, or even a rational one, an empowered and unencumbered electorate is the best remedy to tyranny of any kind, but current circumstances give me no choice but to abandon a position on which I have staked a good portion of my professional life. The atom of ownership is too smashed, and the proxy system through which corporate voting is carried out has been too corrupted to give any hope of a democratic resolution to the multiple ills of corporate governance today.

Toward Meaningful Change

So, what can be done? For starters, the Great and Good of Investing shouldn't have to do all the heavy lifting themselves.

Washington Post business and economics columnist Steven Pearlstein has pointed out that average Americans could go a long way toward improving the behavior of the banking and insurance industry by simply refusing to hand its worst offenders their money.

"If we don't like the rip-out-your-eyeball culture of Wall Street, if we're tired of the inherent conflicts of interest, if we don't want to encourage the excessive leverage and risk taking and executive compensation, we can take our money elsewhere—to companies that deliver as good or better products and services at the same or lower prices. Forget about occupying Wall Street—why not just defund it?" [184]

As Pearlstein points out, mutually owned banks and insurance companies were once commonplace—Ben Franklin launched the first such insurance company in America, the Philadelphia Contributionship, formed in 1752. All that began to change dramatically in the 1960s as both industries consolidated and began stretching, first across state lines, then all over the county and around the world, and finally became intertwined with one another with the end of the Glass-Steagall Act in 1999. But mutual banks and insurance companies can still be found, and their record is in almost every way superior to the conglomerate giants that replaced them.

"Today, mutual banks and credit unions operate more efficiently than their stockholder-owned competitors. They have fewer loan losses and write-offs and have taken on less risk and less leverage. They charge lower fees for their services and lower interest rates for their loans. They loan more of their funds to households and small businesses. They have noticeably better service ratings from customers."

The differences aren't so stark in the insurance industry, Pearlstein writes, because mutuals make up a far bigger share of that market than of banking, but in general they have lower expense ratios, return more of the premium dollars to policyholders, and keep more capital in reserve against losses. "On ratings of overall financial strength, mutuals consistently win out. The big difference comes in the area of customer service, where almost all of the top-rated insurers are mutuals."[185]

The point of distinction here is the same as that between drone and non-drone corporations: ownership. Mutual companies have it by definition—they're mutually owned. The lower their overhead and the better run they are, the more everyone wins—owners and managers. Public corporations are, of course, mutually owned as well, but the proxy system—the supposed pathway to corporate democracy—has been manipulated to precisely the opposite effect. Proxy voting is the moat around management, not the bridge into the castle. Only a select few investors have the clout to alter that equation.

Legislative relief also would help ease the asymmetry between corporate and public power. The DISCLOSE Act championed by Rhode Island Sen. Sheldon Whitehouse—Maryland Rep. Chris van Hollen has introduced a companion act in the House—would shine light into the squirming netherworld of campaign financing.

Corporations and wealthy individuals, as we've seen, can easily hide their political contributions until after the election cycle. Corporations can do so forever if they donate under cover of a trade association such as the U.S. Chamber of Commerce. The DISCLOSE Act would go a long way toward remedying that inevitably pernicious situation by requiring Super PACs, 501(c) groups, trade associations, corporations, and labor unions to report major donors behind expenditures in excess of $10,000 within 24 hours of the outlay. Not surprisingly, the Act has come under heavy attack by the usual corporate protectors and parrots in Congress.

Another measure, the Shareholder Protection Act, would require what seems only commonsensical of publicly traded corporations: that they secure permission from shareholders to spend company resources to influence the outcome of elections and then disclose in a timely fashion just how the money has been spent. This one, too, has come under withering assault, including a July 2010 letter from Business Roundtable Executive Director Larry Burton to Reps. Barney Frank and Spencer Bachus of the House Financial Services Committee that argues, in part:

> By mandating shareholder and board approval of a specific type of expenditure—funds used for political activities—the Shareholder Protection Act of 2010 would involve shareholders in day-to-day corporate operations and place boards of directors in the inappropriate position of micromanaging decisions about the use of corporate funds. This would upset the delicate balance among the roles and responsibilities of shareholders, boards of directors and management . . . . Business Roundtable believes that decisions about how corporations use their financial resources—including whether and how a corporation should allocate funds for political activities—should remain where they are: within the judgment of a corporation's management team, acting under the oversight of a board of directors elected by the corporation's shareholders.[186]

Such an argument might make something approaching sense if that "delicate balance" did exist and if board members were, in fact, democratically chosen in free and open elections instead of largely appointed by CEOs. But really, who's kidding whom? What's more, the worst abuses of campaign financing are likely to occur at precisely those corporations where boards most nearly resemble lap dogs and where the exercise of shareholder ownership is weakest, i.e., drone corporations. Only a select few investors have the power to break through this mountain of nonsense, too, and begin to redress the worst wrongs of *Citizens United*, the most shameful Supreme Court decision of my lifetime.

Another vital area where the Great and Good of Investing could help break an impasse and bring true and lasting order to what has become, in modern times, infinitely convoluted arrangements: fiduciary responsibilities. The law on the matter has a noble lineage, from bank trust statutes to the Investment Company Act of 1940, to the Employee Retirement Income Security Act of 1974, or ERISA, which extended the concept and practice of fiduciary duty to managing pension funds (and with which I am intimately familiar, having served as the Labor Department's Pension Administrator during the Reagan years).

Learned commentary on the law is unambiguous as well. No one has ever expressed it better than Justice Benjamin Cardozo when he wrote that "Many forms of conduct permissible in a workday world for those acting at arm's length are forbidden to those bound by fiduciary ties. . . . Not honesty alone, but the punctilio on an honor the most sensitive is then the standard of behavior. As to this, there has developed a tradition that is unbending and inveterate."

The "punctilio on an honor most sensitive" that Cardozo espoused and 2nd Circuit federal judge Henry J. Friendly upheld eloquently in 1971, in *Rosenfeld v. Black*, was largely overruled by Congress in its 1975 revisions to the Securities Act.[187] The conglomeration of the financial industry has further complicated matters by assuring that those exercising fiduciary duties will be in almost constant conflict of interest with other elements of the same institutions whose interest is in turning a profit, not protecting pensions and pensioners. But surely, that moral obligation still exists, even if the legal understanding has been reduced to slurry.

135

Untangling the two entails somehow sequestering fiduciary obligations from the balance of the functioning of these conglomerate financial institutions, perhaps through free-standing "special purpose trust companies." The options are many, but whatever the best solution, only a select few investors have the power and resources to make it happen, the savvy to fully conceive of how such a separation might be made, and the backbone to push through policy changes that will be fought every step of the way by CEOs who, if they happened to trip over fiduciary responsibilities, would assume it was the office cat.[188]

Conceptually, the most elegant solution to the corporate capture of American polity would be a Constitutional amendment separating Corporation and Government, along the lines of the First Amendment separation of Church and State. Our Founding Fathers recognized that the "more perfect union" they sought required a "great barrier" (Madison's phrase), or a "wall of separation" (Jefferson's), between church and state, both to prevent government from being subservient to religious agendas and to protect religion itself from being corrupted by government. In fact, that's not a bad description of where we have landed today. Government finds itself subservient to corporate clout, wants, and needs; and corporations and their CEOs—the high priests of this secular Church of the All-Consuming Greed—have become corrupted by their ready access to political and regulatory power.

Both sides, in short, would clearly benefit from an Amendment that, to paraphrase Justice Hugo Black, required that government "be neutral among corporations and citizens: it cannot promote, endorse, or fund corporations or specifically corporate interests."[189] But in practical terms, pushing such an amendment through state legislatures even more dominated by corporate interests than the U.S. Congress would prove at the least daunting and quite likely impossible. What's more, any similar solution would need to be implemented globally, across the developed and even semi-developed world, to forestall the inevitable flight to more welcoming sovereigns and more hospitable domiciles. Good luck with that.

A cleaner Constitutional approach would be a simple declaration, in amendment form, that there is no such thing as a "legal person."

136

Such rights as accrue to a person are available only to "natural persons," those born of the union of sperm and egg. This might be effectively framed as protection against artificial life forms already emergent on the far horizon, but the ever-vigilant Business Roundtable is not likely to miss the more immediate threat such an amendment would pose to the legal underpinnings of *Citizens United*.

In any event, the purpose here is not to pinpoint the One Answer to the current crisis of corporate governance but to launch a process by which the answer (or more likely answers) might emerge—a creative tension between those who would protect the status quo and those with the capacity, intellectual and otherwise, to forge a new, as yet undefined way by and through which responsible governance will unleash the full wealth-creating potential of the corporate form. To that end, readers are invited to join the discussion at my website, www.ragm.com. The only bad idea is one that might move the process forward yet never gets expressed.

From Weakness to Strength

One other possibility to throw into the pot:

Jujutsu, the Japanese martial arts form, is based on the principle that it is more effective to use an opponent's force against him than to confront the opponent with your own strength. Jujutsu seems to have been born of necessity—samurai developed it in feudal times to combat armed, often armor-clad enemies. Their only path to victory was to allow the enemy to defeat itself.

Metaphorically, we're at much the same point today in the struggle to contain corporate dominion. Corporations control the high ground. They're armed, armored, and protected by courts and Congress. And to combat them, their opponents have only weaknesses: atomized shareholding, absentee owners, a farcical proxy system, and on and on. Therein I contend lies great opportunity.

Follow me along two converging paths. The first is the strongest link, bar none, in the entire absentee-ownership investment chain:

index funds. Index funds are structurally passive. Since their composition is dictated by the index to which a particular fund is tied, they have little incentive to consider the performance or even the behavior of the companies in which they are invested. This makes index funds, by default if nothing else, among the strongest supporters of drone corporations—and probably the fastest growing. Add together these two factors, structural passivity and rapid growth, and index funds are a drone CEO's dream come true. But index funds are also exactly what enlightened ownership demands: long-term shareholders.

That gets us to the second path: the intense competition to attract investment between different species of funds, those in which actual humans select the stocks and other marketable securities (actively managed), those in which shares are essentially gambling chips moved constantly around the table as dictated by computer codes (algorithm), and the index funds we have just been looking at.

Within this fierce competition, index funds already have one big inherent advantage: low management fees dictated largely by the fact that there is so little to manage. The index itself determines the purchase and mix of securities. Algorithms are low cost as well but, as history painfully shows, always have the potential of going rogue. Actively managed funds like to tout their star stock pickers, but flesh-and-blood expertise doesn't come cheap, and there's little evidence that once you get down to net returns, actively managed funds do any better than or even as well as index funds.

But what if index funds were given one more competitive advantage: a "bonus-dividend" that would build on what they already are—long-term shareholders? Merely possessing shares over a defined time wouldn't be sufficient. Owners would also have to show commitment to act in a meaningful capacity in that role: the will to enforce change when necessary (see the "minimal ownership agenda" at the end of Chapter 7), the competence to know when change is needed *and* when it isn't, and above all else, the motivation, standing, and mettle to hold management to account.

The devil is in the details as always, but a bonus dividend of some sort should be sufficient to focus the index fund managers on what has always been true of the industry though too little realized: that as long-term investors, they must care about governance because from it flows a corporation's plans, focus, strategies, and ultimately sustainable profitability. Active managers dodge the issue, at least in the short term, by selling the stock if they don't like the management. Algorithm traders don't even bother with that; the code does the thinking. But index fund managers can't sell the stock so long as it remains in the relevant index and thus have every incentive to change the management when needed. And that, indeed, is the underlying idea here: to create holistic owners, not ones who snooze through the life of the holding or who focus on single issues like ever-fluctuating share price.

The impediments are many, beginning with the apoplexy of the Business Roundtable and U.S. Chamber of Commerce, and the strength and sway of their lobbying arms. (Make no mistake: Holistic owners would seriously challenge drone hegemony.) Two-tier stock would also have to climb many hills, including the often slippery one of the SEC. Any "show-commitment" requirement would have to be carefully thought out and written air-tight. Otherwise, mischief and even sabotage are certain to sneak in. There are always more excuses not to do something transformative than there are reasons for moving ahead.

Corporations as well would have to be convinced that issuing a bonus dividend rewarding committed, holistic ownership was in their own best interests. That is a steep slope in itself, but the simple fact that owned corporations produce significantly higher total shareholder returns on average than drone ones should be all the incentive index funds need to establish the rules of engagement for such dividends and muscle them past aghast managers and reluctant boards.

And the rewards of creating genuine ownership within every publicly traded company? These, I think, speak for themselves.

- Index funds and their trustees would be attracted by an extra return arising from an ownership pattern to which they are already committed.

- Such a long-term ownership bonus would significantly enhance the competitive stature of passive funds, as against actively managed ones.

- This, in turn, would provide additional revenue with which the index fund industry could afford to finance the infrastructure necessary for a structure of ownership compatible with what I have outlined above.

- Algorithm funds, passively manage themselves, except by the computers that run them, would eventually find ways to cash in as well—it's just code, after all—and active managers would finally come to the table themselves as the industry weight shifted toward holistic ownership.

- And as that happened and the dominance of drones and CEO manager-kings waned, markets would rationalize and perform more efficiently, and human needs would once again find their way back to the center of policy considerations.

That in essence is what this entire book has been about: not destroying the corporation but taming it and harmonizing its vast power with human values. Could there be a higher calling for the Great and Good of Investing than helping to achieve that? Could there be a higher calling for society as a whole, or a greater need?

As investors, as citizens, as heirs of this great American experiment in responsible liberty and capitalist-based democracy, we all have a role to play in the unfolding drama and a huge stake in its outcome. But every movement needs leaders, and no group is better suited to that than the trustees of our flagship foundations and endowments. By embracing their duties and these nascent possibilities, by looking holistically at the corporation not only as a profit machine but as one entity among many in a complex society, trustees will empower the reforming energies gathered on the horizon and bring to a smooth landing a flight that more and more appears to be careening out of control. The choice, really, is up to them.

"Weakness in the demand for responsibility did not derive from the immediate context of that demand but from other undesirable by-products of our utilitarian emphasis," James Willard Hurst wrote four decades ago, "Power continually presented new temptations and shifted into new forms. To structure power for responsibility called for continuing, close attention and an investment of resources of mind and energy which we begrudged. We begrudged the investment because we felt that it subtracted from our primary interest in the economy, which was the main area in which we pursued utility. Thus, though the demand to enforce responsibility upon power was real and valid, we were inclined to fumble in realizing it and to fail in will or insight in implementing it."[190]

The time is right; the need, great. This is the moment to decide.

****

Appendix

Chief Justice Roberts: Judicial Activist for Corporate Power

Robert A. G. Monks and Peter L. Murray
August 2009

One of the phrases bandied about during the confirmation hearings for Judge Sonia Sotomayer's nomination to the United States Supreme Court is "judicial activism" - a tendency of judges to use the cases they decide to implement their own notions of public policy. Of course, all recent Supreme Court nominees have steadfastly denied any shred of judicial activism and have uniformly maintained that the proper role of a judge, even a Supreme Court Justice, is to apply existing law, whether Constitutional, statutory or precedent, to the facts of the case before him or her. No one has been more outspoken against the evils of judicial activism than Chief Justice Roberts.

Now it appears that the Chief may be undertaking a bit of judicial activism of his own. The case is *Citizens United v. FEC*. The conservative group that sponsored *Hillary: The Movie* just before the Democratic primary is seeking to avoid or roll back the 2002 McCain-Feingold campaign finance law that prohibits the use of corporate funds to influence elections. Chief Justice Roberts and his conservative Supreme Court majority are getting ready to use *Citizens United* as the vehicle to overrule established precedent (and overturn carefully drafted legislation) and grant business corporations a constitutional right to use their funds to participate in political debate, not only on public issues, but even in the election of candidates to office. Such a move would be judicial activism on a grand scale!

1. Freedom of Speech for Corporations.

Business corporations and their owners have participated in political life in many ways for many years. Corporate lobbying, campaign contributions by business leaders, "soft money campaign support" by businesses, the "revolving door" of businessmen and public servants: these are only a few of the many ways that corporations interact with politicians and political institutions in an effort to influence public action to their advantage. The American public has learned to live with a strong connection between business and politics.

What is relatively new, however, is the claim that business entities have a *constitutional right* to utilize their economic power to participate in political campaigns and influence the outcome of public votes free of meaningful public regulation. The idea can be traced to the 1978 case of *First National Bank of Boston v. Bellotti*, 435 U.S. 765, where a 5 to 4 majority of the Court[191] voided a Massachusetts law that prohibited corporations from expending funds in connection with state referenda having nothing to do with their business on the ground it was an unconstitutional interference with corporate freedom of speech. In brief, *Bellotti* stands for the principle that corporations may spend money to influence the outcome of a public referendum regardless of whether the issue relates to the corporation's business interests.

Bellotti is the handiwork of Lewis Powell, the consummate corporate lawyer from Richmond, Virginia, who was drafted to the Supreme Court by Richard Nixon in 1971. Although Powell was considered a moderate on most issues during his fifteen years on the Court, he was an activist to the core in matters affecting corporations and their role in American political life. In fact, only two months before he was nominated, the future Justice wrote a secret memorandum to the Director of the U.S. Chamber of Commerce on the vital need of corporate America to take a more direct and powerful role in American politics:

> *But one should not postpone more direct political action,*
> *while awaiting the gradual change in public opinion to*

*be effected through education and information. Business
must learn the lesson, long ago learned by labor and
other self-interest groups. This is the lesson that political
power is necessary; that such power must be assidously
(sic) cultivated; and that when necessary, it must be
used aggressively and with determination -- without
embarrassment and without the reluctance which has been so
characteristic of American business.*

It is thus not too surprising that it was Powell who wrote the Court's opinion sustaining the First National Bank of Boston's constitutional challenge to the Massachusetts statute.

In holding that the First Amendment of the United States Constitution prevents the states from seriously restricting corporations from using their funds to influence the outcomes of political referenda, Powell reached back to a statement reported to have been made by Chief Justice Waite at the outset of oral argument in a 19th Century railroad tax assessment case, *Santa Clara County v. Southern Pacific R. Co.*, 118 U.S. 394, 396 (1886): "The court does not wish to hear argument on the question whether the provision in the Fourteenth Amendment to the Constitution, which forbids a State to deny to any person within its jurisdiction the equal protection of the laws, applies to these corporations. We are all of opinion that it does."

This dictum was in dissonance with the general view that corporations, as artificial creations of the laws of men, enjoyed no "inalienable rights" but only those legal properties that the Legislature chooses to give them. *Belotti*, 435 U.S. at 822-823 (Rehnquist, J., dissenting). While there are numerous cases applying the Due Process Clause of the 14th Amendment to the property of corporations, no case prior to *Bellotti* had suggested that corporations had the rights to freedom of speech, assembly, petition, etc. spelled out in the First Amendment. *Id.*

Justice Powell's discovery (or invention) of First Amendment rights for corporations in *Bellotti* let a genie out of the bottle. Justice Rehnquist, who dissented in *Belotti*, recognized that:

A State grants to a business corporation the blessings of potentially perpetual life and limited liability to enhance its efficiency as an economic entity. It might reasonably be concluded that those properties, so beneficial in the economic sphere, pose special dangers in the political sphere.

Belotti, 435 U.S. at 825-826 (Rehnquist, J., dissenting). Even the *Bellotti* majority acknowledged that allowing corporations to deploy their financial power in elective politics would go too far. In a footnote to the majority opinion, Justice Powell noted that the Massachusetts statute under review also prohibited corporate contributions to candidates or political parties. *Belotti*, 435 U.S. at 787 n. 26. That portion of the statute was not being challenged and Justice Powell noted how important it was for the government to be able to prevent the corruption of elected officials by contributors. *Id*. This footnote left open (perhaps even embraced) the idea that Congress still has the power to curb a corporation's use of its economic power to influence candidate elections.

2. Curbing Corporate Influence on Elections.

History since *Bellotti* has affirmed Justice Rehnquist's foresight. The role of money in politics at all levels has burgeoned.[192] Both states and the federal government have been scrambling to get things under some control. At the state level this struggle has brought forth various forms of campaign finance legislation.

A Michigan law that restricted a corporation's ability to use general corporate funds to influence elections of candidates came before the Rehnquist Court In 1990. In *Austin v. Michigan Chamber of Commerce*, 494 U. S. 652 (1990), a majority of the Court (including Chief Justice Rehnquist) somewhat narrowed the negative implications of *Bellotti* by ruling that the state could prohibit a corporation from spending its own funds in support of a candidate. At the federal level the battle to curb excesses of corporate (and individual) campaign and election spending ultimately resulted in the Bipartisan Campaign Reform Act of 2002, commonly known as "McCain-Feingold" after its Senate sponsors. When Congress crafted the prohibitions of corporate electioneering and related political activity in McCain-Feingold it paid careful attention to Austin and to footnote 26 in *Bellotti*. The reform legislation contained an express prohibition on corporate funding of "electioneering communications" that referred to a political candidate within 30 days of a primary and 60 days of a general election.

McCain-Feingold was immediately tested by a constitutional challenge in a suit by U.S. Senator Mitch McConnell that reached the Supreme Court in 2003. *McConnell v. Federal Election Commission*, 540 U. S. 93 (2003). McCain-Feingold survived the challenge; the Court's decision held that corporate political speech in the form of "issue advertisements" that are the "functional equivalent" of "electioneering communications" can be legally banned without infringing any corporate constitutional rights of freedom of speech .

3. The Roberts Majority and Corporate Influence in Politics.

Enter Chief Justice John G. Roberts, who was confirmed in 2005. During his hearings the new Chief Justice repeatedly referred to the role of a Supreme Court justice as akin to that of "umpire". It now appears that the umpire may be about to change the rules of the game.

In *FEC v. Wisconsin Right to Life Committee*, 551 U.S. 449 (2007), the Wisconsin Right to Life Committee (a nonprofit corporation subject to the limitations of McCain-Feingold) ran ads encouraging viewers to contact Wisconsin's U.S. Senators and urge them to oppose filibusters of Bush administration judicial nominees. The Federal Election Commission deemed the ads to be the "functional equivalent" of electioneering communications and refused to allow them to be aired within 60 days of the election.

The conservative majority of the Roberts Court ruled that the "functional equivalent" test must be applied narrowly, too narrowly to cover the activities of WRL. According to Chief Justice Roberts and his conservative colleagues, unless an ad was reasonably interpreted as urging the support or defeat of a candidate, it was eligible for an "as applied" exception to the McCain-Feingold limits on issue ads close to an election. By construing the statute narrowly, the Court did not have

147

to attack the pre-existing authority of *McConnell* or *Austin*, although Justices Scalia, Thomas and Kennedy were ready and eager to do so. As Chief Justice Roberts observed,

> *McConnell held that express advocacy of a candidate or*
> *his opponent by a corporation shortly before an election*
> *may be prohibited, along with the functional equivalent of*
> *such express advocacy. We have no occasion to revisit that*
> *determination today.*

Wisconsin Right to Life, 551 U.S. at 476 n. 8. The clear implication is that on some "tomorrow" the Court may indeed be ready to overrule *McConnell* and *Austin*. Such a move would unshackle the genie that was first uncorked by Justice Powell in *Bellotti*, and let corporate financial power loose on the election process.

4. *Citizens United* **and the Unshackling of the Genie.**

Citizens United may be the case that the Roberts majority has been waiting for. Since it is hard to imagine that a film about then-presidential candidate Hilary Clinton can "reasonably be interpreted as anything other than an ad urging the support or defeat of a candidate", Citizens United is asking the Roberts Supreme Court to overrule *McConnell* and kill the "functional equivalent" rule that the Rehnquist Supreme Court crafted only 6 years ago.

The case was argued on March 23, 2009. During the argument it became apparent that some Supreme Court Justices may be thinking about the *Citizens United* case as an opportunity to strip away any meaningful restrictions on the ability of corporate America to participate in all aspects of the political process including the election of candidates for public office.[193]

This concern became more concrete when Chief Justice Roberts took the unusual step of setting the case for re-argument on September 9. The order for re-argument specifically invites the parties to address the issue of whether the *McConnell* or *Austin* precedents should be overruled, either in whole or in part. Enter judicial activism

- of the conservative variety.

McConnell and *Austin* are four-square precedents of the
United States Supreme Court that establish limits to the corporate free
speech genie conjured up in *Bellotti*. Important national legislation is
grounded on these precedents. There is no national hue and cry for the
repeal of McCain-Feingold or for overruling the judicial foundation
of its constitutionality. Certainly there is no indication that *Austin*,
McConnell or McCain-Feingold have become obsolete or outdated. In
fact, all indications are to the contrary. With each successive election
the role of corporations and their money is becoming ever more
evident.

Austin, McConnell and McCain-Feingold sought to place
limits on the corporate genie's capacity to do serious mischief on our
political institutions. There is good reason now to fear that the Roberts
majority may be poised to wipe away these limits in an act of judicial
activism that is breathtaking in its implications. Based on the shaky
constitutional bases of *Bellotti*, such a decision by the Roberts majority
would transform the core of our nation's political structure.

a) **The Illegitimacy of** *Bellotti*

As noted before, the sole authority for the proposition that
the free speech rights of the 1st Amendment benefits and protects
corporate entities as well as natural persons is *First National Bank of
Boston v. Bellotti*. At the time the Constitution was originally adopted,
corporations were very rare and special entities, created by legislative
acts for particular described purposes. The word "corporation"
appears nowhere in the Constitution or Bill of Rights. It is scarcely
conceivable that the drafters of the Constitution had anything
resembling corporate entities in mind when they drafted the Bill of
Rights.

For nearly a century it was assumed that the Bill of Rights
protected persons, not corporations. The14th Amendment ban on
deprivation of property without due process or equal protection of
the law has been consistently applied to property of corporations and

natural persons alike. However prior to *Bellotti* there was never any hint that the purely personal rights of the first Amendment of the Bill of Rights belong to corporate entities as well as human beings. As Justice Rehnquist noted in his *Bellotti* dissent, "The question presented today, whether business corporations have any constitutionally protected liberty to engage in political activities, has never been squarely addressed by any previous decision of this court." *Belotti*, 435 U.S. at 822 (Rehnquist, J., dissenting).

The lack of legal foundation for Bellotti together with its disturbing policy considerations have been pointed out in legal literature ever since the case came down in 1978.[194] That the Court may be on the verge of taking a step for which *Bellotti* is the main basis of support demonstrates the lengths to which the Roberts majority is prepared to go to promote corporate "rights".

b) Judge-Made Law and Political Institutions

Judge-made law does not have the democratic legitimacy of measures that have been adopted by legislatures and ratified by executive action. Judges are not legislators. They are not, and should not be, politically accountable to anyone. They do not take part in the political debate concerning the matters that they decide.

The lack of democratic legitimacy for judges and their rulings counsels a degree of restraint in the creation of judge-made law. Such restraint is even more important when judges are confronted with the potential of transforming by their own decisions the structure or function of essential political institutions.

The common law system gives courts the authority to develop rules of law based on accretion of case by case decisions. Such a system has decided strengths in the creation of responsive doctrines of private law governing the legal dealings of private actors with each other. On the other hand, the authority of public law, particularly laws establishing the structure and function of various participants in the political process, derives entirely from the democratic composition of the law-giving body. Widely representative legislative bodies can act to restructure American politics and can be held accountable for their actions in political elections. On the other hand, when courts act to change the political playing field, they are in no way accountable for the havoc that their decisions may wreak. Ever since the founding of the Republic the United States Supreme Court has been conscious of this issue and has refrained from adjudicating issues of political structure and role and has deferred to the democratically constituted legislature in these matters.[195]

Thus, when Justice Roberts and his colleagues consider transforming the American political landscape to the great benefit of corporate business entities, they are on very uncertain ground as far as their basic judicial legitimacy is concerned.

5. Overrule *Bellotti*!

Now that 30 years have passed since Justice Powell took a prefatory comment in a 19th Century railroad case and used it to enfranchise corporations in the political process, events have shown that it is *Belotti*, not the cases that tried to limit its mischief, which should be up for reconsideration. The incredible growth of corporate presence in all forms of political activity has indeed brought about the corruption of the political process that Justice Powell acknowledged might occur if corporate enterprises were allowed to employ their resources to influence the election of candidates. The "problem of corruption of elected representatives through the creation of political debts" has become the American political reality in the 21st Century. Why not put *Bellotti* on the table for reconsideration when the Court convenes on September 9?

Emboldened by *Bellotti*, corporations have indeed taken the program of the Powell Memorandum to heart. The number of registered lobbyists in Washington has increased from 3,400 in 1977 to almost 34,000 in 2006. In the 2008 House and Senate races $400 million dollars was raised and spent for candidates by political action committees, mostly linked to business corporations. Corporate spending for such events as the Inauguration, Party Conventions and even Presidential Debates has become embarrassingly blatant.

A recent study of the relationship of health care industry campaign support to positions of congressmen on health care reform concluded.

> *These findings also point to a need to address the fundamental problem in the financing of American politics. Members of Congress spend time courting donors when they could be passing legislation, building relationships with other lawmakers, or addressing constituents' needs. With ever increasing campaign costs, members follow the infamous bank robber Willie Sutton's advice to go to "where the money is" – the industries regulated by their committees. That only makes the public more skeptical that policy is for sale.*

Advancing Health Care Reform Through the Swamp of $187 Million in Interested Political Money, Public Campaign Action Fund, Released July 2009, available at http://www.campaignmoney.org/node/272173/print (downloaded August 5, 2009).

It is now clear that Justice Powell's judicial activism in Bellotti has not stood the test of time. The notion that artificial legal entities organized to facilitate the transaction of business and the accumulation of wealth should have constitutionally protected rights that the Framers believed came to human beings from their Creator has even less credibility today than in 1978. Certainly the amorality of corporate America has only become clearer since Justice Powell gave corporations political rights. A fair-minded and conservative Court, in tune with traditional values of all Americans, would take the opportunity posed by Citizens United to reconsider the juridical basis on which *McConnell* and *Austin* are being attacked rather than consider overruling these useful and important mainstream precedents. It is instead *Bellotti* that should be overruled to give our public institutions a chance to escape the corruption of corporate money that is overwhelming politics at all levels.

The evident intention of the Roberts Court to undermine, roll back and ultimately overrule the useful *McConnell* and *Austin* precedents is the very kind of judicial activism that Chief Justice Roberts and his conservative brethren have so consistently deplored.

152

In fact, the activism that Justice Roberts is now contemplating goes far beyond even such "activist" decisions as *Roe v. Wade*. The conservative activists of the Roberts Court are poised to turn over the American elective process to the tender mercies of Corporate America. Sadly, it appears that our judicial tradition of constitutional restraint with respect to issues affecting politics may be out the window when an opportunity arises to increase the power and influence of America's corporate entities. The many senators who have expressed concern over judicial activism in the Sotomayer hearings need only look to the Roberts Court on September 9 for an example of judicial activism that will take our breath away.

###

Endnotes

Introduction

1. Adolf A. Berle and Gardiner C. Means, *The Modern Corporation and Private Property,* (New York: Harcourt Brace, 1968), p. 311.

2. "Corruptions Perceptions Index, 2012," Transparency International, http://www.transparency.org/cpi2012/results (accessed January 29, 2013).

3. Malcolm Gladwell, *Outliers: The Story of Success*, (New York: Little, Brown & Company, 2008).

Chapter 1

4. "Outside Spending," Open Secrets, http://www.opensecrets.org/outsidespending/ (accessed January 27, 2013).

5. Lee Fang, "Never Mind Super PACs: How Big Business Is Buying the Election," *The Nation*, August 29, 2012.

6. "Outside Spending," Open Secrets (accessed January 27, 2013).

7. "John Boehner," Open Secrets, http://www.opensecrets.org/ (accessed January 27, 2013).

8. Lisa Graves, "A CMD Special Report on Funding and Spending," *PR Watch* (blog), July13, 2011.

9. "Donor Stats," Open Secrets, http://www.opensecrets.org/

(accessed January 27, 2013).

10. Mark Sherman, "Samuel Alito, Supreme Court Justice, Takes on Citizens United Critics," *Huffington Post*, November 17, 2012.

11. Robert G. Kaiser, *So Much Damn Money*, (New York: Random House Digital, 2009), pp. 343-44.

12. Fang, "Never Mind Super PACs…"

13. Joseph Kahn, "Cheney Refuses to Release Energy Task Force Records," *New York Times*, August 4, 2001.

14. Matthew Mosk, et al., "Romney Party Yacht Flies Cayman Islands Flag," *ABCNews*, August 29, 2012.

15. Lawrence Mishel and Natalie Sabadish, "CEO pay and the top 1%: How executive compensation and financial-sector pay have fueled income inequality," Economic Policy Institute (Issue Brief #331), May 2, 2012.

16. "Q&A with Mihir A. Desai: Compensation Practices & Incentives," *Harvard Magazine*, September-October, 2012.

17. Daniel Gross, "Bye-Bye Pension!" *Slate*, January 27, 2006.

18. Edward Wyatt, "Judge Blocks Citigroup Settlement with S.E.C.," *New York Times*, November 28, 2011.

19. Henry Blodget, "Meanwhile, the Fed's Still Paying Banks Not to Lend," *Business Insider*, March 12, 2012.

20. Sarah Anderson, Chuck Collins, et al., *The CEO Hands in Uncle Sam's Pockets*, Institute for Policy Studies, August 16, 2012.

21. Nicholas Shaxson, *Treasure Islands,* (London: Vintage Books, 2012).

22. Peter Schroeder, "Rep. Bachus tells local paper that

Washington should 'serve' banks," *The Hill*, December 13, 2010.

23. Beth Healy, "Fidelity hails SEC backtrack on money market funds," *Boston Globe*, August 23, 2012, and Nathan Hale, "Money market fund reform looks dead in the water," *CBS News*, August 30, 2012.

24. "Regulators Captured," *Wall Street Journal*, August 23, 2012.

25. Daniel Kaufmann, "Corruption and the Global Financial Crisis," *Forbes*, January 27, 2009.

26. Matt Taibbi, "How Wall Street Killed Financial Reform," *Rolling Stone*, May 10, 2012.

27. Hedrick Smith, "When Capitalists Cared," *New York Times*, September 2, 2012.

28. Thomas B. Edsall "Is Poverty a Kind of Robbery," *New York Times*, September 16, 2012.

Chapter 2

29. *Spencer Stuart Board Index*, http://www.spencerstuart.com/research/bi (various years for United States, 1998-2011).

30. "Majority Voting for Investors," Council for Institutional Investors, http://www.cii.org/majority_voting_directors (undated).

31. Lucian A. Bebchuk, "The Myth of the Shareholder Franchise," (Harvard Law School Discussion Paper No. 567, 11/2006, revised 03/2007); since published in *Virginia Law Review*, Vol. 93, No. 3, pp. 675-732, 2007.

32. Peter Drucker, "The Bored Board," in *Toward the Next Economics and Other Essays*, (New York: Harper & Row, 1981).

33. Securities and Exchange Commission, "S.E.C. Adopts New

Measures to Facilitate Director Nominations by Shareholders," press release, August 25, 2010, http://www.sec.gov/news/press/2010/2010-155.htm.

34. *Business Roundtable and Chamber of Commerce of the United States of America v. Securities and Exchange Commission*, 647 F.3d 1144 (DC Circuit Court of Appeals, 2011).

35. Resolution submitted to Exxon Annual Meeting, 2002, http://www.ragm.com/library/Resolution-submitted-Exxon-Annual-Meeting-2002 and S.E.C. response to proposal to separate CEO and Chairman, 2002.

36. Suzanne Kapner, et al., "Citigroup Investors Reject Pay Plan," *Wall Street Journal*, April 17, 2012.

37. Dionne Searcy "Was Justice Kennedy's Opinion on Citizens United Uninformed?" *Wall Street Journal*, October 27, 2010.

38. Robert A.G. Monks and Nell Minow, *Corporate Governance*, (West Sussex: John Wiley & Sons, 2011).

39. Sir William Blackstone "Of Corporations," in *Commentaries on the Laws of England, 1765-1769* (book 1, chapter 18).

40. Monks & Minow, *Corporate Governance*.

41. Theodore Roosevelt, "Progressive Covenant with the People," (speech, August 1912).

42. Theodore Roosevelt, *An Autobiography*, (New York: Charles Scribner's Sons, 1913), p. 557.

43. *Liggett Co. v. Lee*, 288 U.S. 517 (1933) 565.

44. *Ibid.* pp.565-567.

45. Adolf A. Berle and Gardiner C. Means, *The Modern Corporation and Private Property*, (New York: Harcourt Brace, 1968)

p. 64.

46. Charles Lindbloom, *Politics and Markets: The World's Political-Economic Systems*, (New York: Basic, 1977).

47. Berle and Means, *The Modern Corporation*, p. 8.

48. General Electric Company – Major Holders, *Yahoo! Finance*, http://finance.yahoo.com (accessed January 27, 2013).

49. General Electric Company – Historical Prices, *Yahoo! Finance*, http://finance.yahoo.com (accessed January 27, 2013).

50. Felix Salmon and Jon Stokes, "Algorithms Take Control of Wall Street," *Wired*, December 27, 2010.

51. Nathaniel Popper, "Knight Capital Says Trading Glitch Cost it $440 Million," *DealBook* (blog), New York Times, August 2, 2012.

52. General Electric Company – Major Holders, *Yahoo! Finance*, http://finance.yahoo.com (accessed January 27, 2013).

53. "401(k) plan fee disclosure form for services provided," U.S. Department of Labor, Employee Benefits Security Administration, (accessed January 27, 2013).

54. Chrystia Freeland"Capitalism without the Capitalists," *New York Times*, December 22, 2012.

55. *Citizens United v. F.E.C.*, 558 U.S. (2009).

Chapter 3

56. Edward Jay Epstein, *Who Owns the Corporation: Management vs. Shareholders*, (New York: Priority Press Publications, 1986).

57. Charles Gasparino and Paul Beckett, "How John Reed Lost the Reins of Citigroup to His Co-Chairman," *Wall Street Journal*, April 14,

2000.

58.   "Nursery School Scandal," *ABC News*, December 6, 2002.

59.   "No Line Responsibilities," *Wall Street Journal*, December 8, 2008.

60.   Robert Scheer, *The Great American Stickup: How Reagan Republicans and Clinton Democrats Enriched Wall Street While Mugging Main Street,* (New York: Nation Books, 2010). Also, "The Long Demise of Glass-Steagall," and "Mr. Weill Goes to Washington," Frontline, PBS, May 8, 2003.

61.   Eric Jackson, "Should CEOs Sit on Other Companies' Boards?" *SeekingAlpha* (blog), April 23, 2009.

62.   "Former Citigroup CEO Says 'Break Up the Megabanks,'" *Common Dreams*, July 25, 2012.

63.   "Sandy Weill sells his NYC apartment for jaw-dropping sum," *Investment News*, December 19, 2011.

64.   "Executive PayWatch," AFL-CIO, http://www.aflcio.org/ Corporate-Watch/CEO-Pay-and-the-99 (accessed December 1, 2012).

65.   Natasha Singer, "In Executive Pay, A Rich Game of Thrones," *New York Times*, April 8, 2012, and "Executive pay stop the bubble bursting," HR Future, http://www.hrfuture.net/cover-story/executive-pay-stop-the-bubble-bursting.php (accessed January 29, 2013).

66.   James Warren, "Berkshire Hathaway Shareholder Meeting: The Takeaway," *Huffington Post* (blog), May 7, 2012.

67.   Ha-Joong Chang, *23 Things They Don't Tell You About Capitalism*, (New York: Bloomsbury Press, January 17, 2012).

68.   Gary Burtless, "The Financial Crisis and a Flaw in Corporate Capitalism," *Brookings Institution* (blog), March 17, 2009.

69. "The Top 10 Highest-Paid CEOs, Chief Executive Officers 2012," *TheRichest.org* (blog), October 30,2012. See also, "Executive PayWatch," AFL-CIO.

70. *Ibid.*

71. Jacqueline Palank, "Ex-Kodak Employees Blast Bonus Plan," *Wall Street Journal*, July 25, 2012.

72. Mike Wood, "Mike Zafirovski seeks $12 million payout from Nortel," *Total Telecom*, October 12, 2009.

73. Mihir Desai, "The Incentive Bubble," *Harvard Business Review*, March 2012.

74. Robert A.G. Monks, *Corpocracy*, (Hoboken, NJ: John Wiley & Sons, 2008), pp. 65-67.

75. Sarah Anderson, Chuck Collins, et al., *The CEO Hands in Uncle Sam's Pockets* , Institute for Policy Studies, August 16, 2012, and David Kocieniewski, "Tax Breaks From Options a Windfall for Business," *New York Times*, December 30, 2012.

76. Jeff Madrick, "Sandy Weill, King of the World," in *Age of Greed: The Triumph of Finance and the Decline of America, 1970 to the Present*, (New York, Vintage, June 12, 2012).

77. Edward Jay Epstein, *Who Owns the Corporation: Management vs. Shareholders*, (New York: Priority Press Publications, 1986), p. 41.

78. Daniel Fisher, "The Most Outrageous Executive Perks," *Forbes*, June 27, 2012.

79. Jim Edwards, "The 33 Richest People in Advertising, Ranked by Income," *Business Insider*, May 19, 2012.

80. Brad Hamilton, et al., "Citi's Sky-High Arrogance: Company Jet for Mogul's Luxe Holiday," *New York Post*.

81. Josh Levs, "Big Three auto CEOs flew private jets to ask for taxpayer money," *CNN.com*, November 19, 2008.

82. Daniel Fisher, "The Most Outrageous Executive Perks," *Forbes*, June 27, 2012.

83. *Ibid*.

84. John Schiffman, et. al., "The lavish and leveraged life of Aubrey McClendon," *Reuters*, June 7, 2012.

85. Geraldine Fabrikant, "G.E. Expenses for Ex-Chief Cited in Filing," *New York Times*, September 6, 2002.

86. Paul Hodgson and Greg Ruel, *Twenty-One U.S. CEOs with Golden Parachutes of More Than $100 Million*, (GMIRatings, January 2012), http://origin.library.constantcontact.com/download/get/file/1102561686275-69/GMI_GoldenParachutes_012012.pdf.

87. Robert Brokamp, "Jack Welch's Very Golden Years," *Motley Fool*, September 9, 2002.

88. The Business Roundtable letter to the Securities and Exchange Commission, February 23, 201, "BRT Letter on Application of ERISA Fiduciary Rules to Proxy Advisory Firms," http://businessroundtable.org/news-center/brt-letter-on-application-of-erisa-fiduciary-rules-to-proxy-advisory-firms/ and Martin Lipton, "Harvard's Shareholder Right Program Is Wrong," Harvard Law School Forum on Corporate Governance, March 23, 2012, https://blogs.law.harvard.edu/corpgov/2012/11/30/harvards-shareholder-rights-project-is-still-wrong/.

89. Daniel Brooksbank, "Chevron Seeks DiNapoli's Correspondence on Shareholder Resolutions," *Responsible Investor*, November 20, 2012.

90. Simon Billenness, "An Analysis of the Financial and Operational Risks to Chevron Corporation from *Agunda v. ChevronTexaco*," Report Commissioned by Oil Change International,

2012, and Nichola Groom, "Chevron accuses NY State comptroller of ethics breach," *Reuters*, November 20, 2012.

91. Steven Greenhouse "Here's a Memo from the Boss: Vote This Way," *New York Times*, Oct. 26, 2012.

92. Caleb Melby, "Breaking Down Centi-Millionaire'Papa' John Schnatter's Obamacare Math," *Forbes*, November 12, 2012.

93. "Papa John's Obamacare Costs Are Far Less Than Price of Free Pizza Giveaway," *Huffington Post*, November 13, 2012.

94. Caleb Melby, "Breaking Down Centi-Millionaire'Papa' John Schnatter's Obamacare Math," *Forbes*, November 12, 2012.

95. *Citizens United v. F.E.C.*, 558 U.S. (2009).

Chapter 4

96. Felix Salmon "Bob Rubin's Legacy," *Reuters*, September 20, 2012.

97. Michael Beckel, "Lobbyists' Newest Target in Wall Street Reform Battle? Federal Oversight Agencies," *Open Secrets* (blog), November 11, 2010.

98. Matt Taibbi, "How Wall Street Killed Financial Reform," *Rolling Stone*, May 10, 2012.

99. Eric Lipton, "Congressional Charities Pulling In Corporate Cash," *New York Times* (Politics blog), September 5, 2010.

100. Bill Allison, "Congressional Charity Begins on K Street," *Sunlight Foundation* (blog), July 12, 2011.

101. Robert A.G. Monks and Peter Murray, "Chief Justice Roberts: Judicial Activist for Corporate Power," August 19, 2009 (see appendix). See also: Corpocracy: How the CEOs and the Business

Roundtable Hijacked the World's Greatest Wealth Machine – And How to Get it Back, (Hoboken, NJ: John Wiley & Sons, 2008).

102. Lewis Powell to Eugene B. Sydnor, Jr., August 23, 1971, "Attack on American Free Enterprise System." Lewis S. Powell, Jr., Archives, Washington and Lee University School of Law, http://law.wlu.edu/powellarchives/page.asp?pageid=1251.

103. "About Agency," State of Delaware, Department of State, Division of Corporations, http://corp.delaware.gov/aboutagency.shtml (accessed November 29, 2012), and Nicholas Shaxson, *Treasure Islands*, (London: Vintage Books, 2012) p. 140.

104. Shaxson, *Treasure Islands*, p.143.

105. *Ibid*. p. 141.

106. Gretchen Morgenson, "Pequot Capital and Its Chief Agree to Settle S.E.C. Suit for $28 Million," *New York Times*, May 27, 2010, and "S.E. C. Settles With Former Lawyer," June 29, 2010.

107. Matt Taibbi, "Why Isn't Wall Street in Jail?" *Rolling Stone*, February 16, 2011.

108. Richard Heinberg, *The End of Growth: Adapting to Our New Economic Reality*, New Society Publishers, 2011.

109. Elliott Freeman, "Ron Paul condemns close ties between FDA and big pharma," *Digital Journal*, April 11, 2012.

110. "Canada pulls out of Kyoto protocols," *CBCNews*, December 12, 2011.

111. Chris Mooney, "Some Like it Hot," *Mother Jones*, May/June, 2005.

112. Mooney, "Some Like it Hot," and Oriana Zill de Granados, "The Doubters of Global Warming," *Frontline*, PBS, (accessed January 19, 2013).

113. Clifford Krauss, "Halliburton Moving C.E.O. From Houston to Dubai," *New York Times*, March 12, 2007.

114. Chris Hedges, *Empire of Illusion: The End of Literacy and the Triumph of Spectacle*, (New York, Nation Books, 2009), p. 66.

115. Mark Sweeney, "Martin Sorrell prepares to move WPP headquarters back to London," *Guardian*, August 30, 2012.

116. Shaxson, *Treasure Islands*, p.23

117. "Enough Food for Everyone," enoughfoodif.org, (accessed January 19, 2013).

118. Rana Foroohar, "Companies Are the New Countries, *Time*, February 13, 2012.

Chapter 5

119. Charles Duhigg and Keith Bradsher, "How the U.S. Lost Out On iPhone Work," *New York Times*, January 22, 2012.

120. *Ibid.*

121. Clyde Prestowitz, "Apple makes good products but flawed arguments," *Foreign Policy* (blog), January 23, 2012.

122. Business Roundtable "Roadmap for Growth," December 8, 2010 at 3, http://businessroundtable.org/studies-and-reports/roadmap-for-growth/.

123. *Ibid.* (multiple pages)

124. Eileen Appelbaum "No Happy Ending for Friendly's," *Huffington Post*, November 21, 2011.

125. Quoted in *When Corporations Ruled the World*, by David Korten, (Kumarian Press and Barrett-Koehler Publishers, 1995) p. 83.

126. Laurel Adams, "EPA Superfund cleanup costs outstrip funding," *Center for Public Integrity* (blog), February 22, 2011.

127. Helaine Olen, "Who Killed Hostess Brands and Twinkies," *Forbes*, November 16, 2012.

128. Erica Kelton, "More drug companies to pay billions for fraud, join 'dishonor roll' after Abbott settlement," *Forbes*, May 10, 2012.

129. Carolyn Hoyos, "BP battles to clear its Augean stables," *Forbes*, September 20, 2006, and U.S. Chemical Safety Board, "U.S. Chemical Safety Board Concludes "Organizational and Safety Deficiencies at All Levels of the BP Corporation" Caused March 2005 Texas City Disaster That Killed 15, Injured 180," March 20, 2007.

130. James A. Baker, et al., "The Report of the BP U.S. Refineries Independent Safety Review Panel," January 2007 (copy accessed at ProPublica.org, November 2012).

131. Robert A.G. Monks and Nell Minow, *Corporate Governance*, (West Sussex, John Wiley & Sons, 2011), pp. 450-1.

132. Jason Ryan, "BP Agrees to $4.5 Billion Gulf Spill Settlement, 3 Former Employees Charged," *ABCNews*, November 15, 2012.

133. Business Roundtable "Roadmap for Growth," December 8, 2010 at 24, http://businessroundtable.org/studies-and-reports/roadmap-for-growth/.

134. "Another Slap on the Wrist," New York Times, January 19, 2013.

135. Abram Chayes quoted in Ralph Nader and Mark J. Green, *Corporate Power in America*, (New York: Grossman Publishers, 1973), vii.

Chapter 6

136. Ric Marshall, "Passive Investing and Indexed Companies," GovernmentCapture.com, (accessed February 15, 2013).

137. Business Roundtable, "Members," (accessed January 27, 2013).

138. Marshall, "Passive Investing and Indexed Companies."

139. *Ibid*.

140. Marshall, "Passive Investing and Indexed Companies."

141. *Ibid*.

142. Tamara Keith, "Bank Overcharged Military Families on Mortgages," NPR, January 19, 2011, and Shayndi Raice and Nick Timiraos, "U.S. Sues Wells Fargo for Faulty Mortgages," *Wall Street Journal*, October 10, 2012.

143. Adam Hartung,"Oops! Five CEOs Who Should Have Already Been Fired," *Forbes*, May 12, 2012.

144. Marshall, "Passive Investing and Indexed Companies."

145. Marshall, "Passive Investing and Indexed Companies."

146. *Ibid*.

147. "Big No Tax Corps Just Keep on Dodging," Citizens for Tax Justice, April 9, 2012, http://ctj.org/ctjreports/2012/04/big_no-tax_corps_just_keep_on_dodging.php.

148. David Evans, "When drug makers' profits outweigh penalties," *Washington Post*, March 19, 2010.

149. Klaus Kneale and Paulo Turchioe, "Layoff Tracker: Number of layoffs since Nov. 1, 2008, at America's 500 largest public companies," *Forbes*, (accessed January 29, 2013).

150. *Ibid.*

151. Jackie Tortora, "Where Did All Our Pensions Go?" www.afl-cio.org October 7, 2012.

152. Carrick Mollencamp and Bret Wolf, "HSBC Agrees to A Record $1.9 Billion Fine In Money Laundering Case," *Huffington Post*, December 11, 2012, and David Enrich and Jean Eaglesham, "UBS to Pay $1.5 Billion to Settle Libor Charges," Wall Street Journal, December 20, 2012.

153. Marshall, "Passive Investing and Indexed Companies."

154. "The SIPRI Top 100 arms-producing and military services companies, 2010," Stockholm International Peace Research Institute, http://www.sipri.org/yearbook/2012/05 (accessed January 18, 1013), and ownership data from Morningstar, (accessed January 28, 2013).

Chapter 7

155. Freedom-Group.com (accessed January 10, 2013).

156. Michael D. Shear and Adam Nagourney, "Reaction to Newtown Shootings Spreads to Corporate America," *New York Times*, December 18, 2012, and Greg Roumeliotis and Sakthi Prasad, "Newtown backlash prompts Bushmaster Rifle sale," *Reuters*, December 18, 2012.

157. "CalSTRS says reviewing private equity gun investment," *Reuters*, December 17, 2012.

158. "The Fight for Fossil-Fuel Divestment," *Harvard Magazine*, December 14, 2012.

159. George Draffan, "Multimillion Dollar Fines and Settlements Paid By Corporations," *Endgame.com*, (accessed January 29, 2013), and Phineas Baxandall and Ryan Pierannunzi, "Subsidizing Bad Behavior: How Corporate Legal Settlements for Harming the Public

Become Lucrative Tax Write Offs, with Recommendations for Reform," U.S. PIRG Education Fund, (accessed January 19, 2013) and other data maintained at www.uspirg.org.

160. Donald L. Bartlett and James B. Steele, *Betrayal of the American Dream*, (New York: Public Affairs, July 31, 2012).

161. Ric Marshall, "Passive Investing and Indexed Companies," GovernmentCapture.com, (accessed February 15, 2013).

162. "Vanguard Group Is Increasing Its Positions In These Stocks," *SeekingAlpha.com*, February 3, 2012, and "State Street Corporation at Goldman Sachs Financial Service Conference Transcript," AlacraStore.com, (accessed January 11, 2013).

163. Nell Minow,"An Interview with Warren Buffett," GMIRatings video on YouTube, part six of nine, September 2010, (accessed January 11, 2013).

164. "Who Owns Pfizer?" Stockzoa.com (accessed January 11, 2013).

165. "Pfizer's Ex-Chief to Get Full Retirement Package," *New York Times*, December 22, 2006.

166. I've written more about this—and BP failures to fix the problems first noted after Texas City—on my blog, "Déjà vu All Over Again: British Petroleum," www.ragm.com, June 20, 2011.

167. Mary Williams Walsh, "I.B.M. to Freeze Pension Plans to Trim Costs," *New York Times*, January 6, 2006.

168. "Our Investment Philosophy," Gates Foundation website, (accessed January 11, 2013).

169. "Bill and Melinda Gates Foundation," whalewisdom.com (accessed January 14, 2013).

170. Tomio Geron, "CalPERS Returns 1% for Fiscal Year," *Forbes*,

July 16, 2012.

171. "Widening Gap Debate," Pew Center on the States, Issue Brief, (Pew Charitable Trusts, 2012), p. 5.

172. "Gun Company Investors Include Teachers' Retirement Funds," *Huffington Post*, December 17, 2012.

173. "Top 25 university endowments," MarketWatch.com, February 2, 2012.

174. Rob Kozlowksi, "Endowment execs top pay list for tax-exempt institutions," *Pensions & Investments*, November 7, 2011.

175. "Top U.S. Foundations by Asset Size," www.foundationcenter. org, (accessed January 11, 2013).

176. "Slow Growth for Largest Pension Funds," Towers Watson, September 5, 2012, http://www.towerswatson.com/assets/pdf/7857/ PI300_2011.pdf.

177. Christopher Condon and Sree Vidya Bhaktavatsalam "Fink Leverages BlackRock's $3.5 Trillion in Shareholder Push," *Bloomberg*, January 19, 2012.

178. "Amgen Gets a Gift From Congress," *New York Times*, January 1, 2013.

179. Donald J. Munro, *Ethics in Action: Workable Guideline for Private and Public Choices*, (Hong Kong: The Chinese University of Hong Kong, 2008).

Chapter 8

180. James R. Lowell, "Once to Every Man and Nation," *Boston Courier*, December 11, 1845.

181. Elisabeth Bumiller, "Readying the Slingshot for a Modern

Goliath," *New York Times*, June 12, 1998.

182. Louise Armistead, "BlackRock's Michelle Edkins behind wave of shareholder revolts," *Telegraph*, May 4, 2012.

183. Chrystia Freeland, "Self-Destruction of the 1%," *New York Times*, October 13, 2012, and *Plutocrats: The Rise of the New Global Super-Rich and the Fall of Everyone Else*, (The Penguin Press HC, October 11, 2012).

184. Steven Pearlstein, "Occupy Wall Street? Just Defund It," *Washington Post*, Saturday, December 1, 2012.

185. *Ibid.*

186. Business Roundtable, "Letter to Barney Frank and Spencer Bachus on the Shareholder Protection Act," July 18, 2010, http://businessroundtable.org/news-center/letter-to-barney-frank-and-spencer-bachus-on-the-shareholder-protection-act/.

187. An Act to Amend the Securities Exchange Law of 1934...Pub. L. 94-29, 89 Stat. 97, (1975).

188. With apologies to E.B. White who expressed the same thought much better when addressing the political predations of the McCarthy Era.

189. *Everson v. Board of Education of the Township of Ewing*, 330 U.S. 1, (1947).

190. James Willard Hurst, *The Legitimacy of the Business Corporation in the Law of the United States, 1780-1970*, (University of Virginia Press, 1970) p. 59.

Appendix

191. The majority opinion was written by Justice Powell, who was joined by Justices Stewart, Blackmun, and Stevens. Chief Justice

Burger concurred in the decision but wrote separately. Dissenting were Justices Rehnquist, White, Brennan, and Marshall.

192. In the 1976 Presidential campaign, concluded shortly before the Court handed down a decision in Bellotti, the candidates spent about $66.9 million dollars. In the 2008 Presidential campaisn, the candidates spent about $1.3 billion dollars. Center for Responsive Politics at http://www.opensecrets.org/pres08/totals.php?cycle=2008 (downloaded August 5, 2009).

193. Corporate Money and Campaigns, New York Times Editorial (March 24, 2009) available at http://www.nytimes.com/2009/03/24/opinion/24tue2.html (downloaded August 5, 2009).

194. See, e.g., J. Skelly Wright, Money and the Pollution of Politics: Is the First Amendment an Obstacle to Political Equality?, 82 Col. L. Rev. 609 (May 1982).

195. A notable exception to this policy of restraint was Bush v. Gore, 531 U.S. 98 (2000) in which the Rehnquist Court intervened in the Florida election process in a manner that gave George W. Bush the 2000 presidential election.

About the Author

Pioneering shareholder activist and corporate governance adviser Robert A.G. Monks has written widely about shareholder rights & responsibility, corporate impact on society and global corporate issues.

He is the author of *Corporate Governance* (with Nell Minow), Power & Accountability (with Nell Minow), *Watching the Watchers*, *The New Global Investors*, *The Emperor's Nightingale*, *Corpocracy* and *Corporate Valuation* (with Alexandra Lajoux).

Mr. Monks is an expert on retirement and pension plans and was appointed director of the United States Synthetic Fuels Corporation by President Reagan, who also appointed him one of the founding Trustees of the Federal Employees' Retirement System. Mr. Monks served in the Department of Labor as Administrator of the Office of Pension and Welfare Benefit Programs having jurisdiction over the entire U.S. pension system.

Mr. Monks was a founder of Institutional Shareholder Services (ISS), now the leading corporate governance consulting firm. He also founded Lens Governance Advisers and co-founded GMIRatings (formerly The Corporate Library). He is a shareholder in and advisor to Trucost, the environmental research company.

Mr. Monks was a featured part of the documentary film, *The Corporation*, and was the subject of the biography, *A Traitor to His Class* by Hilary Rosenberg.

For more information

http://ragm.com

Twitter

@bobmonksnews

Facebook

https://www.facebook.com/pages/Robert-Monks/76370086412

Acknowledgements

I, alone, am responsible for the contents of this book. As is well known, writing a "short" book is hard, so you will understand that this book required the collaborative effort of four people – Nell Minow, partner for going on thirty years and publisher, who has improved all on which we have worked together; Ric Marshall is a polymath who made his genius available – especially in Chapter Six which represents his intellectual work product, Stephanie Philbrick who has organized us all and insisted that we document accurately all statements of fact – bless her. Howard Means has exceeded any standard of which I am aware in being able to extract from a rather violent mass of material and emotion a text that is a pleasure to read and a profit to understand.

During all of the sixty some years of my professional life, I have been blessed with partners. Many have helped in the preparation of this book. Since 1956 Dwight Allison's intellect, decency and persistence have improved my life, and so he persists with his welcome enthusiasm for this effort. This book is in one respect a progress report on the pamphlet – Capitalism Without Owners Will Fail - that Allen Sykes and I wrote ten years ago. Alas, it is an account of our failure to elicit adequate concern over "mute" ownership. My college roommate and lifelong friend, Professor Donald J. Munro has taught me of the nuances between guilt and shame which inform the conclusions I reach in this book. All who are concerned with the problems of inappropriate exercise of power in the United States owe a debt of gratitude to my law school classmate Ralph Nader whose integrity in the pursuit of "legitimate citizenship" has illumined our generation. Ralph manages to find the time to make supremely helpful textual suggestions. Sir Adrian Cadbury unfailingly gives of his time and insight to those who ask for it. Again, his generosity, especially in tightening my references to economics, has made this book better. Jack Bogle has had a keen sense of fairness in making available the fruits of American business wealth to investors; he has insisted on this ... to the point of giving away upwards of $20 billion to the investors in Vanguard. Beyond this, he is a fine scholar (and I gratefully accept his corrections) and a fearless commentator. Charles Handy has written so well over the whole spectrum of issues surrounding the role of business in society, only a few of which this book addresses, that his suggestions were particularly welcome. David Korten has "been in the belly of the beast" and is today's great aspirational teacher of what should and can be. I thank him for cogent commentary on what is. Hazel Henderson is perhaps the most successful non-economist to make sense out of economics with a remarkable touch for communication through imagery. Adam Frost works in this field and is a searcher for solutions so his comments are personal and, therefore, most valuable. Alexandra LaJoux possesses a dazzling range of artistic talents, in the exercise of one of which she wrote a book with me. Her support and insight are so helpful. Eleanor Bloxham kindly gave me several hours of textual review of the manuscript – any author knows how rare and welcome that kind of generosity is. Thank you. Rick Bennett has shared so much of this journey with me and will ultimately express its conclusions. Howard Sherman has devoted his professional life to the corporate governance field and his perspective is a welcome addition. Jim McRitchie has contributed "the" organizing blog for work in the corporate governance field. He has the honesty and impatience to break through the fog that surrounds much discussion of the rights of members of the corporate constellation. Dr. Kimberly Gladman combines scholarship and patience with those who might push the boundaries of where factual analysis properly leads. Larry Alexander, long time business book editor for Wiley, and the literary father of my CORPOCRACY has generously continued to help with editorial comments and personal contacts, but his greatest contribution is enthusiasm. Lev Janashvili has devoted a significant portion of his career in trying to improve my capacity to communicate to various publics. Neva Goodwin has personally been concerned with developing an Economics that makes sense for the future, so she provides a balanced perspective to my passion. Paul Lee has long been my "go to" person with questions and ideas about this entire field – he is the best scholarly source there is. I have benefitted from several years of conversations with Paula Gordon and Bill Russell about the range of ideas in this book. Their friendship and persistent interest has helped me a great deal. Simon Wong writes well. I look forward to reading what he will say about global governance in the years to come. Sam Wohns belongs to a distinguished lineage of Harvard people – starting with Brandeis – who are concerned with the problems of institutional integrity. Gareth Shepherd has unique insight into how corporate governance failures correlate with loss of market value.

I am also grateful to:

Allen White, Anna Bernasek, Arn Person, Bill Lerach, Bob Massie, Charles Elson, Frank Partnoy, Gavin Grant, Jesse Norman, Jeff Gramlich, John Plender, John Richardson, Joy Howell, Linda Hirsch, Lucian Bebchuk, Mac Van Wielengen, Raj Thamotheram, Rolf Carlsson, Sandra Guerra, Simon Walker.